Lincolnshire Echo

Big Skies Over Lincolnshire

Bygone Memories from Bomber County

Compiled by
Peter and Pat Washbourn

DB
PUBLISHING

First published in Great Britain in 2001 by
The Breedon Books Publishing Company Limited
Breedon House, 3 The Parker Centre, Derby, DE21 4SZ.

This paperback edition published in Great Britain in 2013 by DB
Publishing, an imprint of JMD Media Ltd

ISBN 978-1-78091-346-9

Printed and bound in the UK by Copytech (UK) Ltd Peterborough

Contents

Introduction

To many people, Lincolnshire is a flat county. In reality, it has the highest ground above sea level in the east of England.

It does not have mountains or high hills and this factor was instrumental in choosing a title for this book, hence *Big Skies Over Lincolnshire*.

The subtitle, Bygone Memories from Bomber County says it all. It is, in the main, a collection of photographs taken from the archives of the *Lincolnshire Echo*, with the addition of a few from private collections.

Flying has taken place in Lincolnshire for almost 90 years. The first flights into the city of Lincoln took place in 1912. With the outbreak of war two years later, military flying arrived, in the form of Royal Naval Air Service and Royal Flying Corps 'flight stations'. In 1918, they were amalgamated into the Royal Air Force.

During World War Two, there were 48 airfields in Lincolnshire. All but a few were bomber stations, so it is obvious why the county earned its 'Bomber County' nickname. Today, there are only four active airfields still in use, although flying still takes place from others, by commercial and private aircraft.

The photographs in *Big Skies Over Lincolnshire* cover the period from 1930 to the mid-1970s, with just a few from outside these parameters.

Pictures of aircraft are interspersed with pictures of events at a number of the RAF stations. Ranks and titles in captions are those which were current when the photographs were taken.

Also included are memories from individuals, who served with the Royal Air Force. In addition, there are memories from two former *Lincolnshire Echo* staff photographers who worked side-by-side for 35 years and took many of the pictures.

The final chapter is dedicated to the members of the Royal Air Force who lost their lives in serving their country. There are many memorials, not only located at former air bases but also in numerous locations around the county and a selection of these cover the wide variety which can be found.

Producing this book could not have been done without the help of many people. Special thanks must go to the individuals who agreed to be interviewed or provided information about the memories.

Early pictures of flying in Lincolnshire have come from the collection of Bill Baker and our thanks go to him for allowing access.

Thanks also to Russell Kirk, at the *Lincolnshire Echo* for help in locating and printing some of the photographs.

And finally, we would like to thank our son, Ian, who is currently serving in the Royal Air Force, at RAF Waddington, for reading through the proofs of this book.

Peter & Pat Washbourn
Summer, 2001

From Humble Beginnings

It is less than one hundred years since man took to the skies in a heavier-than-air machine, the Wright brothers flying their Kitty Hawk at North Carolina on 17 December 1903.

Nine years later, Lincoln had its first taste of aviation when William Hugh Ewen flew into the city and promptly crashed his biplane.

However, it was soon repaired by a local motor dealer and he was able to give a demonstration. Two weeks later, Bentfield Charles Hucks came to Lincoln, but because of bad weather, his aircraft arrived by train. He then, over the next few days, enthralled crowds with his flying displays.

He was to visit Lincoln many times and on one occasion, in 1914, flew his monoplane between the West Towers and Central Tower of Lincoln Cathedral.

World War One saw an increase in flying in the county with the Royal Naval Air Service and the Royal Flying Corps operating from 'flight stations' as they called the airfields.

During the 1914-18 war, many aircraft were built in Lincoln, by both Shuttleworths and Rustons and it was a Ruston-built aircraft which is credited with bringing down the first German invader to be shot down over England. This was a Zeppelin and the action earned the Victoria Cross for the Ruston plane's pilot.

It was in 1918 that the Royal Air Force was formed and in the following years, before World War Two, many types of aircraft were seen in the skies over Lincolnshire.

These included Hinaidi, Hawker Harts, Handley Page Heyfords, Westland Wallace, Hawker Audax and the Avro Tutor.

Many non-stop long-distance record attempts started at RAF Cranwell and these often involved Fairey Napier aircraft, which were virtually flying petrol tanks. They carried two pilots and had sleeping accommodation so that one pilot could rest while the other took the controls. If the plane deviated from its course, a signal buzzer sounded next to the resting pilot to warn him that something was wrong.

And there was one event which would prove to be the forerunner of the 'At Home' and Open Days held at air bases in the second half of the century. This was Empire Air Day and was held at RAF Cranwell.

This then, was the beginning from which Lincolnshire became known as 'Bomber County'. There are forty eight airfields on a map of Lincolnshire in World War II. Four were bombing and gunnery ranges, on the coast and one, RAF Digby, was a Battle of Britain station.

On the day that war was declared, in September 1939, RAF College, Cranwell, closed and re-opened as the RAF College Service Flying Training School, with satellite airfields at Harlaxton and Grantham.

Grantham had quite a line in name changes. Originally RAF Spittlegate, it was renamed RAF Grantham in 1928 and renamed again in 1944, when it became RAF Spitalgate, because of other military establishments in the Grantham area.

William Hugh Ewen was the first pilot to fly into Lincoln, in July 1912, in his Caudron biplane. On landing in a field off the Wragby Road, his wheels caught in a wire fence and his plane landed upside down. Mr Ewen suffered a sprained ankle and his plane was repaired by Gilberts, at their Melville Street premises. (Bill Baker collection)

Bentfield Charles Hucks brought his Bleriot monoplane to the city just weeks after William Ewen made his visit. The plane arrived by train and was transported by road to the West Common, for flying displays. This was the first of many visits to Lincoln by the aviator. (Bill Baker collection)

The Handley Page monoplane which was flown by Ronald Whitehouse in Lincoln in 1913. (Bill Baker collection)

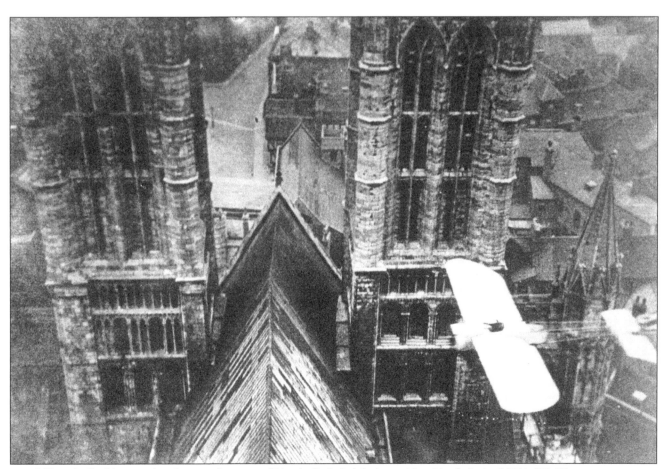

Bentfield Hucks flies his monoplane between the towers of Lincoln Cathedral during a visit to Lincoln in April 1914. (RI–98)

Sir Alan Cobham entertained many with his 'Cobham Circus' between 1932 and 1935. It visited Lincoln and is pictured here flying over the area of Burton Road and Yarborough Road. (RI–505)

The first Ruston-built aircraft which was piloted by Capt Tennant, in 1915. Ruston's produced their 1,000th aeroplane in January 1918 and by the end of World War I, had produced 2,750 aircraft, 3,200 engines and spares for a further 800 engines.

The first Ruston aircraft, a B.E.2c biplane, based on a Sopwith pattern, receives close scrutiny after its first flight.

The 1,000th Ruston-built aircraft, on 4 January 1918, with workers assembled in front of the aircraft.

Training on a radial engine at RAF Digby, in 1935. (RI–945)

Numerous attempts at non-stop long-distance flying records started from RAF Cranwell in the 1920s and '30s. Many of these involved Fairey Napier monoplanes which had a huge wingspan and were capable of flying non-stop for three days and nights. (RI–944)

This diminutive aircraft is a Flying Flea, photographed at RAF Digby in 1936. They were not factory-produced, but intended for the do-it-yourself market. It's wing-span was 20 feet and it weighed 200 lbs. (RI–507A)

A line up of Hawker Hart aircraft, at Waddington, in 1937. First flown in 1928, as a day bomber, a trainer version was also produced in 1932. (RI–739)

Hawker Hart aircraft being refuelled at RAF Digby in 1935 (RI–942)

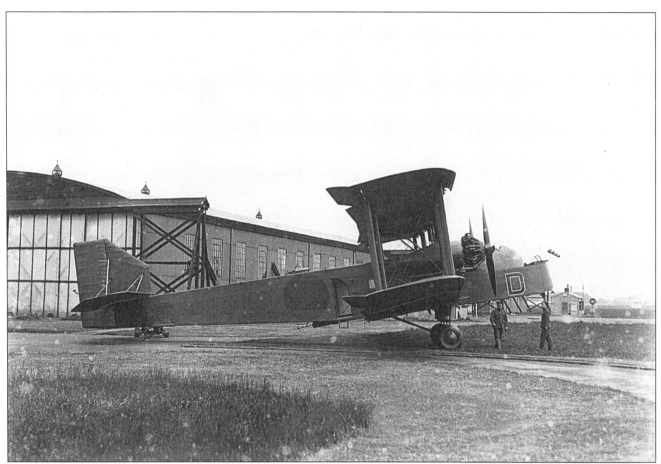

A Handley Page Hinaidi of 503 (County of Lincoln) Squadron, Special Reserve, preparing for take-off at RAF Waddington, in 1934. (RI–506)

On the ground and in the air, Hanley Page Heyfords at RAF Scampton. (RI–738B)

Handley Page Heyfords lined up at RAF Scampton in 1936. (RI–738B)

Hangars and control tower at RAF Waddington, photographed in May 1937. The aircraft are Hawker Harts. (RI–946)

Developed from the Westland Wapiti, the Westland Wallace was used by both the Royal Air Force and the Army. (RI–568)

A mixture of aircraft lined up in front of the hangars at RAF Digby in 1935. (RI–488)

On display at the Empire Air Day, at RAF Cranwell in 1938, a Whitley bomber, with a Blenheim in the background. (RI–612)

A Vickers Wellesley medium-bomber which carried its bomb load in a pannier under each wing. It remained in service until late 1942. (RI–612)

A pair of Hawker Audax aircraft on a low level flight at Empire Air Day at RAF Cranwell in 1938. (RI–612)

A fly past by nine Hawker Harts at Empire Air Day in 1938. (RI– 612)

A familiar sight over Lincolnshire in the 1930s was the Avro Tutor. This particular aircraft is now preserved in the Shuttleworth Collection, at Old Warden Aerodrome. It served with RAF Cranwell from 1933-6 and carries the crest of the Royal Air Force College on its tail-fin.

Nev Needham's Memories

Nev Needham

Nev Needham's days in the Royal Air Force were spent as a National Serviceman after being a member of an Air Training Squadron. Nev was lucky, his 'posting' was just down the road, at RAF Waddington and he has some interesting and amusing anecdotes of his two years as one of the 'Boys In Blue'.

I was fortunate to start an early interest in the Royal Air Force by becoming a member of the ATC City of Lincoln 204 Sqdn.

We had a camp at Linton-on-Ouse which had a squadron of Hornet fighters stationed there and what a glorious aeroplane that was. This very fast piston-engined fighter was a development of the famous Mosquito, it had all the virtues of its forerunner and was faster and easier to handle, though the top speed in those days was restricted, but it could do over 400mph in level flight.

I had my first flight there. We were doing some cleaning jobs when a sergeant pilot came up and asked if anyone fancied giving him a hand in the station Anson? The Anson was a MkI with wooden fixed pitch propellers and as we found out, hand cranked landing gear and hand pumped flaps. That was where the help came in. We flew to Driffield, just up the road and picked up some spares. That was when we found that landing was very interesting, winding down the wheels and pumping the flaps. The pilot took us back the scenic route, with a few turns on the way, our stomachs somewhere back over Driffield. My first official flight was in a de Havilland Rapide. We all did some plotting of the course and I managed to get us over the North Sea. It should have been York! Whoops!

In 1955, as I was an apprentice, I did not go into the forces (for National Service) until I was 21 and of course knew it all! Oh Yes? I arrived at Cardington and was kitted out – one of them, two of those, what size? That size, sign here! I did not know what I had got, but I had signed for them.

Then on to Hednesford. Get out of that nice bus you 'orrible people you! I do not intend to go over that period, except to say that when an NCO said jump, we jumped. I became a marksman with a .303 rifle, sixpence a week extra for that.

It was quite a relief to get to Weeton to train as a piston engine fitter and I enjoyed my time there, actually getting to start and run an aeroplane, in my case a Miles Magister, a training aeroplane and to then get a posting, Waddington!

It was quite a different world to be on a squadron. I saluted everything that moved for a start, then the blokes in the squadron took pity on me and I was soon into the swing of RAF life. Now I was a piston engine trained fitter so what was I doing at an RAF station which had jet-propelled aircraft? The squadron was equipped with Canberras. Well, a great bloke by the name of WO Jukes sorted that out very quickly. I was sent to No3 Bay to serve on the crash crew and service ground equipment.

There, I met Cpl Fred Rayner, a veteran and he taught me all the

An Avro Anson is towed along the A15 from Bracebridge Heath to RAF Waddington for testing.

ropes, bar none. I leaned how to start Canberras and the basic services needed, also how to tow aircraft with a tractor. That ensured me of a place in the servicing flight, if you could tow an aircraft correctly, you had a spot. The Crash Crew side was an education, we were a Master Diversion Unit, so any aeroplane in difficulties was diverted to us.

The very first aeroplane I worked on was an Airspeed Oxford. Ever tried cranking a car to start it? Well, try an aeroplane! You stood on the mainplane and two of you 'wound like the clappers'. You made sure that a plug change had been done.

I also remember when Anson's arrived from the Avro works at Bracebridge Heath. They were towed along the Sleaford road to be tested by the ground staff before being test flown. The OC Bomber Command's Anson had its own little kitchen bar and a loo! Guess who had to empty the Elsan?

The first time we were called out was for a Hunter fighter without all of the hydraulics working. We were soon to get to know that problem. The Hunter landed safely without us chasing it up the runway, he took to the grass which slowed him down quickly for a safe shut down and we towed him back to the hanger, for a repair job to be done.

We than had, at reasonable intervals, a Meteor with a foreign pilot training at Cranwell, who abandoned ship,

15 Flight, at Hednesford, with Nev Needham third from right on the middle row. The corporal, in the middle of the front row, was Cpl Browning, a senior drill instructor from RAF Cranwell.

so to speak, jumping from the Meteor leaving the guns set to fire and the running to the tower. Fred Rayner stopped anyone from going near the aeroplane until he had set everything to safe! A Lincoln Bomber, without any hydraulics, hence no brakes, stopped with its nose pointing over the fence on the Sleaford road end of the runway. A USAF twin-boom freighter, with only one engine, good landing and nice to meet the ground grew. Free cigarettes, get to use their scooters. They made WO Jukes blow a fuse or two. Not the most observant of discipline and they dared to dirty his hanger floor!

Send for Nev and Fred, who cleaned it up with trichlor-ethylene. Makes you very happy if you get a whiff of that, better than a few beers!

We had two Canberras in circuit with frozen wheels, 21 and 27 and both decided they could get an aeroplane up, even though it was freezing, or below, on the ground. We got them down but one with a badly dented nose.

One memory that remains with me, very vividly, was a Canberra opening his throttles for take-off when I noticed that the battery door was open, so I ran on to the runway and signalled the pilot to throttle back whilst I closed the door. I got a thank-you from the CO for that one.

I also remember how we were instructed to prepare to park four Sea Venoms and duly positioned ourselves, one of us on the perimeter track, with three 'erks' on the parking pans. The Venoms taxied to the first batman, who signalled it to come to his pan, but he was horrified when they all began to turn to him. Then they folded their wings and parked. Guess who was that first batman marshaller?

RAF Waddington

The first military flying took place at RAF Waddington in November 1916, when the station opened as a flying training unit, a role in which it continued until the end of the war.

There were many changes in the years between the two world wars with many different types of aircraft.

In 1937, No 44 Squadron became the the first squadron at RAF Waddington to re-equip with the Bristol Blenheim MkI, which was in turn superseded by the Handley Page Hampden bomber. During the Battle of Britain, these aircraft assisted in bombing the invasion barges anchored in the English Channel ports.

The Hampden was replaced by the Avro Manchester, which in turn was superseded by the vastly superior Avro Lancaster.

No 44 (Rhodesia) Squadron received these aircraft on Christmas Eve 1941. After a trial period, the aircraft flew into action in April 1942 and Squadron Leader John Nettleton earned the Victoria Cross whilst leading an attack on a U-boat engine factory.

After the war, RAF Waddington's role was as one of 'care and maintenance' and the base was prepared for the arrival of the V bombers. The 6,000 feet long runway was extended to 9,000 feet.

The Queen gave her approval for the Station Badge, which incorporates the central tower of Lincoln Cathedral. After the Freedom of the City of Lincoln was granted to RAF Waddington, all RAF Waddington aircraft carry the city's Coat of Arms as part of their colour scheme.

In June 1955, RAF Waddington opened as a Master Diversion Airfield and Nos 21 and 27 Squadrons moved in with Canberra bombers. The first operation squadron with Vulcan bombers was No 93 Squadron, in May 1957 and by 1961, the RAF Waddington Vulcan Force was complete and comprised of Nos 44, 50 and 101 Squadrons.

With the introduction of the Tornado bomber, the Vulcans were gradually phased out, but this programme was interrupted by the Falkland Islands conflict and one Vulcan from the base bombed the runway at Port Stanley.

After the war with Argentina had ended, Vulcan aircraft were modified for in-flight refuelling to support the airbridge between Ascension Island and the Falklands.

In 1984, just when RAF Waddington was planning the disbandment of No 50 Squadron, a new unit arrived with the planned introduction of the Nimrod, in an Airborne Early Warning role. But this plan was changed and the Boeing E-3D Sentry aircraft was chosen instead. There were seven of these 'eye-in-the-sky' 'planes operating with No 8 and No 23 Squadrons.

RAF Waddington also became the home of No 51 Squadron equipped with Nimrod R1 aircraft in an electronic reconnaissance role.

In addition to the resident flying squadrons, the airfield was used by a wide range of aircraft types, from several nations, or training exercises and in recent years has expanded to take in the Electronic Warfare and Avionics Detachment, from RAF Wyton and elements of the Air Warfare Centre. No 26 Squadron, RAF Regiment, a ground based air defence squadron, operating Rapier Field Standard C equipment is another recent arrival at Waddington, from RAF Laarbruch.

Crew of a Hampden bomber arrive back safely in Lincolnshire, after a raid in March 1940. (RI–487)

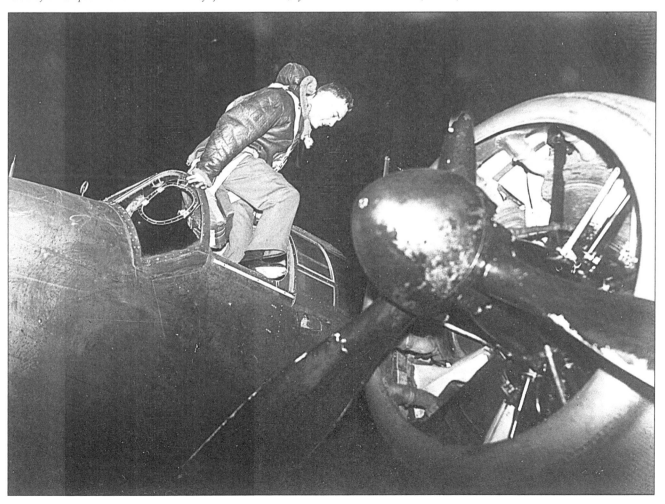

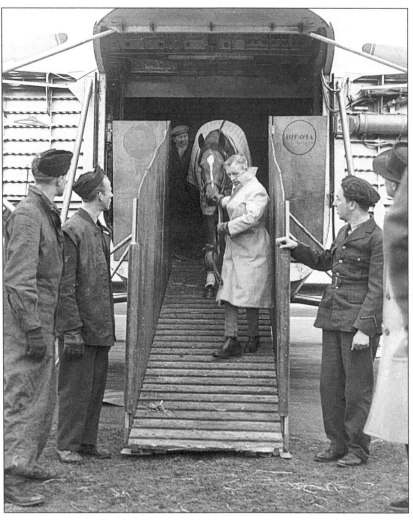

French race horse Astromonte arrives by air at RAF Waddington for the 1951 Lincolnshire Handicap. Owned by the Comte de Chambure, it was unplaced in the race. (RI–949)

Two Vulcans from 83 Squadron, RAF Waddington, took part in a goodwill tour of Argentina, in 1958. Crews are pictured arriving back at Waddington. (RI–3575)

Members of Glasgow University Air Squadron spent their summer vacation of 1952 at RAF Waddington. (RI–950)

Bad weather is always a threat to flying and in January 1963, blowers were used to clear the runways of snow at RAF Waddington. (RI–1380)

A Hunting Jet Provost trainer, a familiar sight in Lincolnshire's skies, at RAF Waddington in 1964. (RI–278X)

A flypast of four Lockheed Shooting Stars at RAF Waddington, in 1964. (RI–2536)

Visitors taking interest in an English Electric Lightning, at RAF Waddington in 1964. (RI–2538)

A flypast by four English Electric Lightnings, at RAF Waddington, in 1965. (RI–964)

Mayor of Lincoln, in September 1964, Coun. Stan Woolhouse and City Sheriff, Mr Stan Williams, with the Mayoress and Sheriff's Lady, travel from Lincoln to RAF Waddington's Open Day by helicopter. (RI–2332)

Five Dutch Airforce F101's in formation at RAF Waddington, in 1965. (RI–964)

An Avro Shackleton flies low over the control tower at RAF Waddington, in 1965. (RI–964)

A chance for visitors to take a close look at an Avro Vulcan at RAF Waddington's At Home Day, in 1958, to commemorate the 18th anniversary of the Battle of Britain. (RI–2330)

An opportunity for young visitors to sit in a gun turret at RAF Waddington in 1958. (RI–2330)

Enthusiasts taking a close look at the aircraft line up at RAF Waddington in 1959. (RI–4143)

A flypast by six USAF jets at RAF Waddington's At Home Day in 1963. (RI–2337)

A Boeing Superfortress in a tanker role, refuelling a trio of planes from the United States Air Force, at Waddington in 1963. (RI–2337)

Wing Commander Arthur Griffiths, Officer Commanding 101 Squadron, at RAF Waddington, in 1963, with crews who flew non-stop to Australia in Vulcan bombers in 18 hours. (RI–2187)

When the Vulcans returned to Waddington, the aircraft sported a kangaroo emblem, to remind the crews of their trip. (RI–2335)

Visitors to RAF Waddington's At Home Day, in 1959, waiting to take to the sky for a pleasure flight. (RI–4143)

Visitors to RAF Waddington's At Home Day, in 1963, looking at a visiting aircraft from the USAF. (RI–2336)

Crowds at the At Home Day, at RAF Waddington, in 1959, watch a low-level run by an Avro Vulcan B1. (RI–4143)

Three Vulcan bombers from RAF Waddington travelled to Florida to take part in the USAF Strategic Air Command's bombing, navigation and reconnaissance competitions in 1957. It was the first time in five years that the RAF had taken part in the competition. (RI–2333)

Vulcan bombers carried the City of Lincoln crest on their tail fin when they went to America. (RI–2333)

The RAF's only flying Lancaster prepares to take to the skies again in 1967, RAF Waddington's Golden Jubilee year. (RI–2646)

Station Commander at RAF Waddington, Group Capt Arthur Griffiths carries out last minute checks before taking off in the Lancaster for an air test. It was the first time the aircraft had flown since it was announced two years earlier that 'It would not fly again.' (RI–2646)

Air brakes up and trailing a braking parachute, this Vulcan lands at RAF Waddington during a rehearsal for At Home Day in 1965. (RI–4144)

Lancaster PA 474 was a new arrival at RAF Waddington in 1965. It was painted in 44 Squadron colours and given the code letters KM – B (which it retained until 1979) for the station's Battle of Britain At Home Day. (RI–4144)

PA474 at RAF Waddington shortly after its arrival in 1965. (RI–4144)

A moment of relaxation during rehearsal for the At Home Day. (RI 4144)

50 Squadron, RAF Waddington held a Families Day in May 1966, when there was an English Electric Lightning and a Dominie small jet transport plane on display. (RI–963)

Visitors looking at a model of a Vulcan B2 at RAF Waddington's At Home Day in 1959. (RI–4143)

A flypast by three Avro Shackletons at Waddington in 1959. (RI–4143)

Displaying at Neighbours Day, at RAF Waddington, in 1958, is a Gloster Meteor. The Meteor was the only Allied jet fighter to see service in World War II, just beating the German ME262 into service. (RI–3464)

The Vulcan making a low level pass at RAF Waddington in 1974. (74 – 2 – 560)

Guests at Neighbours Day, at RAF Waddington, in 1958, look at the City of Lincoln coat of arms, which has been carried on all Waddington's aircraft, since 1956. In 1959, the station was granted the Freedom of the City. (RI–3464)

Guests pose for a picture beside a Vulcan B1 at Neighbours Day, at RAF Waddington in 1958. (RI–3464)

A fairly rare visitor to RAF Waddington, was this Blackburn Buccaneer, at Waddington in 1974. (74 – 2 – 560)

The Folland Gnat aircraft of the Red Arrows aerobatic team look almost like models, as they taxi past the Avro Lancaster in 1974. (74–2–560)

Relaxing on the grass, these visitors to RAF Waddington, in 1961, have an Avro Vulcan for a close neighbour. (RI–2545)

Thrilling the crowd at Battle of Britain open day, at RAF Waddington, in 1961, are a Hawker Hurricane and a Supermarine Spitfire. (RI–960)

Contrasts: A Royal Aircraft Factory SE5A, dating from World War I, in contrast with an Avro Vulcan, at RAF Waddington, in 1961. (RI–960)

The Avro 504K was introduced during the time of the Royal Flying Corps, before the RAF was formed in 1918. Crowds at RAF Waddington, in 1963, had a chance to see this veteran aircraft. (RI–2336)

A giant of an aircraft, a Lockheed C-130 Hercules, of the United States Air Force, on display at RAF Waddington, in 1963. (RI–2336)

RAF Waddington At Home Day visitors in 1963 take a close look at an English Electric Lightning. (RI–2338)

Prominent in this picture taken at RAF Waddington, in 1964, is a Handley Page Victor, many of which were used as tankers for in-flight refuelling. (RI–2539)

A chance for visitors to RAF Waddington, in 1963 to look around the inside of a USAF C-130 Hercules. (RI–2338)

Visitors looking at a McDonnell F101 at RAF Waddington's Battle of Britain open day in 1960. (RI–3503)

A chance to look at the mid-upper turret of an Avro Lancaster, at RAF Waddington in 1961. (RI–2545)

Young visitors getting the chance to sit in a cockpit at RAF Waddington's Battle of Britain open day in 1960. (RI–3503)

Plenty of aircraft to catch the attention of visitors to the Battle of Britain open day at RAF Waddington, in September 1960. On display are an Avro Vulcan, Handley Page Victor and Vickers Valiant, plus a Douglas DC3 (Dakota), a Lockheed Starfighter and an English Electric Canberra. (RI–3503)

Visitors to the Battle of Britain open day at RAF Waddington, in 1960, looking at a Tiger Moth. (RI–3503)

The Royal Air Force's last three Avro Lincoln bombers make a final flight over Lincoln, in March 1963. (RI–741)

Echo chief photographer Ken James, flew in a RAF Waddington based Avro Vulcan, in 1962, when the aircraft was refuelled by a Victor tanker in mid-flight. (RI–961)

An air-to-air picture of a Victor tanker in-flight refuelling an Avro Vulcan bomber in 1962. (RI 967)

Flying low down the runway at RAF Waddington, is a Vickers Valiant, with underwing fuel tanks. (RI–278X)

A trio of English Electric Canberra bombers fly over RAF Waddington, in 1964. (RI–2537)

Three Avro's in one picture. The Shackleton frames a Lancaster and Vulcan at RAF Waddington, in 1964. (RI–278X)

Introduced during World War II, the Avro York was a transport aircraft which remained in service for many years and was even used for carrying VIP passengers. This one was photographed at RAF Waddington during an open day. (RI 439)

Young visitors to RAF Waddington, in 1964, meet an American airman. Did they ask 'Got any gum – chum?' (RI–2538)

A Fairy Gannet, with folded wings was an unusual sight at RAF Waddington's 'At Home' day, in 1964. (RI–2538)

Two Navy aircraft at RAF Waddington in 1964. A Fairey Gannet, with its twin propellers and a Sopwith Pup, which was of the type used by the Royal Naval Air Service in World War I. (RI–278X)

An impressive view of an Avro Vulcan, as it displays at RAF Waddington, in 1961. (RI–2544)

Flying over uphill Lincoln, in 1965, (Lincoln County Hospital is on the left) is the RAF's last flying Lancaster, on route from Henlow to RAF Waddington. (36Z)

The crew of Lancaster PA474 who flew the aircraft from Henlow to Waddington, on 18 August 1965. (36Z)

The Lancaster with an Avro Vulcan in the background attracts the attention of many photographers upon arrival at RAF Wadddington in 1965. (36Z)

Air Vice-Marshal Peter Horsley, Air Officer Commanding No 1 (Bomber) Group, inspects personnel at RAF Waddington during his annual inspection in 1971. (N612)

The RAF Pipe Band play at the Air Officer Commanding's inspection in 1971. (N612)

Five survivors of a wartime crash, met up again at RAF Waddington in 1970. Pictured beneath the nose of a Lancaster bomber were left to right Ron Goebel, Haydn Price, Henry Denton, Ted Kneebone and Wilf Hartshorn. (L294)

Their first meeting since the incident, they presented a painting to RAF Waddington. (L294)

The Royal Air Force Aerobatic Team, the Red Arrows, flying Folland Gnat aircraft, flew into RAF Waddington in May 1971. (O–28)

Red Arrow pilots line up in formation in front of one of their Folland Gnat aircraft at RAF Waddington, in 1971. (O–28)

A new servicing system was introduced at RAF Waddington in 1975 and members of 44 Squadron are pictured with their squadron badge. (Y578)

Editor of the Lincolnshire Echo *Frank Shelton, flew with a crew from RAF Waddington to Malta in 1967. He is pictured undergoing last minute tests before flying in an Avro Vulcan. (RI–3151)*

Frank Shelton (left) with the Vulcan crew. (RI–3151)

Boarding the Vulcan prior to the trip from RAF Waddington to Malta. (RI–3151)

Ken James' Memories

Ken James.

Ken James worked as a photographer with the Ministry of Defence for three years and then as a wedding, portrait and industrial photographer before entering the world of newspapers.

I arrived at the *Echo* as a photographer in 1960 and covered a large variety of assignments as expected of a provincial newspaper photographer, until my retirement in March 1995.

One of the memorable things during my time as a photographer on the *Echo* was the amount of flying I became involved in. I loved the flying. All the air views of the villages and towns, the last flights of the Vulcan and Lightnings, flying with the Rothman aerobatic team, gliders, hot air balloons and of course the Lancaster bomber.

I was fortunate to be in the right place at the right time, living at Waddington during the Vulcan era. Also having a very understanding editor (Mr Frank Shelton).

The first flight I had in a Vulcan was for an in-flight refuelling, from Waddington over Scotland. Later I was given the chance to fly with a 101 Squadron crew on an exercise in Australia. We flew via Cyprus, Masira, Ghan, Singapore and on to Darwin.

A 44 Squadron Vulcan on the snow covered runway at Goose Bay. In the background are USAF tanker aircraft.

After the warm trip I was asked if I would like to go on a cold one, a survival exercise with a crew from 44 Squadron, to Goose Bay in Canada. Cold it certainly was, 40 below. Anyway I survived.

My next trip was a wet one, I was dumped into the North Sea in a one man dinghy and when the helicopter hovered to pick me up, the rescuer on the end of the winch asked if I was Ken James. I was then told that they had another assignment so I

All at sea. Ken James drifting in the North Sea, waiting to be 'rescued'.

was left to be picked up later by an Air-Sea Rescue launch from Bridlington. I think I was set up.

One of my most memorable pictures was that of the City of Lincoln Lancaster and an Avro Vulcan flying side by side over Lincoln, with the cathedral in the picture.

My last trip in a Vulcan was when we took a 617 Squadron aircraft down to South Wales to be scrapped during the run down period. They were all excellent trips for a 'civilian'.

Ken James, right, with Aborigines during his visit to Australia with 101 Squadron.

RAF Scampton

RAF Scampton's history starts in World War I even before the formation of the Royal Air Force in 1918.

It began life as a fighter airfield as part of the Royal Flying Corps' 33 Squadron which had its headquarters at Gainsborough, with flight stations at Elsham, Kirton Lindsey and Brattleby.

When the airfield was reopened in 1936, it became RAF Scampton, although it could have been Brattleby or Aisthorpe. It is located almost equidistant from all three villages.

Within six hours of the declaration of war in September 1939, Hampden bombers from Scampton went off on their first raid and among their pilots were flying officers Roderick Learoyd and Guy Gibson, both later to be awarded the Victoria Cross. This highest award for valour was also given to Sergeant John Hannah, also based at Scampton.

Scampton was the home, for a while, of 617 Squadron and it was from here that Lancaster bombers took off from grass runways to bomb the dams on the River Ruhr, in Germany led by Wing Commander Guy Gibson.

Nineteen planes took off to attack the Eder, Sorpe and Möhne dams. Three returned because of mechanical problems but the remaining sixteen flew on and with the special 'bouncing bombs', invented by Barnes Wallis, breached the Möhne and Sorpe dams. But the losses were high. Eight out of the 16 planes failed to return. 617 Squadron then moved, after one more raid, to RAF Woodhall Spa.

The grass runways proved unsuitable for the heavier loads which the bombers were now carrying, so for a year, Scampton was quieter while concrete runways were constructed and it reopened in October 1944, as the home of 153 Squadron. However, it was used by training schools and when the runways were installed, was used by 1960 Bomber Defence Training Flight.

Two stories to come out of Scampton are both from 153 Squadron days. One concerns a WAAF who was smuggled out on a raid, in a Lancaster, who was curious to know what it was like to go on a raid over Germany. This incident was kept secret for many years. The other incident was when a 1,000lb bomb, being dropped during an attack on Cologne, fell through the wing of another Lancaster flying at a lower height. Fortunately, the bomb had fallen an insufficient distance to set the fuse and despite a large hole in the wing, the aircraft flew on, bombed its target and returned 'safely' to base.

After the war, Scampton became home to American B29 Superfortress', during the Berlin airlift, then Lincoln and Canberra bombers before the introduction of the Avro Vulcan, which saw 617 Squadron return to the base with these aircraft. 83 Squadron also returned, they had flown Hampden bombers from Scampton at the start of the war.

Scampton went on to become the home of the Central Flying School and the Red Arrows display team.

It closed in 1995, the School and Red Arrows going to RAF Cranwell, but just before Christmas 2000, RAF Scampton reopened, to the delight of many, as the home once again of the Red Arrows.

Recruits arriving at RAF Scampton which opened for service in 1936. (RI–736)

Paintings of two of RAF Scampton's winners of the Victoria Cross were unveiled when Frederick Handley Page (left) presented portraits of Sergeant John Hannah (second right) and Squadron Leader Rod Learoyd (right). Both recipients of the VC were flying Handley Page Hampdens when they won the award. (RI–750)

Three former prisoners-of-war take a nostalgic look at a Lancaster and two of its huge bombs during a visit to RAF Scampton, in 1975. Left to right, Tom Baker, of Sleaford, John Clarke, of Bracebridge Heath and Paul Hur, of Lincoln. (Z–82)

A wartime Hawker Hurricane caught the interest of youngsters when it flew into RAF Scampton in September 1974. (X–50)

A Horsa glider touches down at RAF Scampton in May 1974. These gliders had been used for many years for troop movements. (RI–966)

A combined exercise was held in 1961, with RAF Scampton taking part in Exercise Mayflight, which was Bomber Command's name in the exercise, with Matador being Fighter Command's name. Air Marshal Sir Kenneth Cross (right), Air Officer Commanding-in-Chief of Bomber Command, pictured with one of the Vulcan crews. (RI–3909)

A line up of Vulcan bombers at Exercise Mayflight. (RI–3909)

Air Vice-Marshal Sir John Whitley, controller of the RAF Benevolent Fund, with Group Captain Richard Wakeford, commanding officer of RAF Scampton in 1964. (RI–3033)

RAF Scampton said goodbye to its station commander, Group Capt Allen Mawer, in January 1968. A pipeband accompanied his departure from the base. (RI–2913)

A jeep, disguised as a Vulcan, tows a mock Blue Steel missile, to take Group Capt Mawer from RAF Scampton. (RI–2913)

Group Capt Mawer had a canopied seat on a 'missile' when he departed from RAF Scampton for a new post at the Imperial Defence College, in London. (RI–2913)

Squadron Leader D.R. Howard in the cockpit of a Canberra bomber before setting off from RAF Scampton on a flight to Cyprus, a distance of 2,200 miles which was completed in 4 hours and 32 minutes. It was the first stage of a training flight to Negombo, Ceylon (now Sri Lanka). The round trip, of 14,130 miles was made in 27 hours 10 minutes flying time at an average speed of 476 mph. (RI–951)

Vulcan crews enjoying a 'cuppa' before setting off on a round the world flight to mark the opening of Rongotal Airport, New Zealand, in 1959. (RI–3029)

The Vulcans, from 617 Squadron at RAF Scampton, prepare for take-off for their visit to New Zealand. (RI–3029)

Crews line up before setting off from RAF Scampton, in 1954 for a goodwill mission to West European and Mediterranean countries. (RI–2911)

Engines fire up for the tour, nicknamed 'Whitley's Circus', which was led by Air Vice-Marshal John R. Whitley, air officer commanding No. 1 Group, Bomber Command. (RI–2911)

Twenty-seven Squadron members with their green toy elephant mascot, Jumbo. (RI–2911)

A Canberra from 27 Squadron makes a low pass for the benefit of photographers, before setting off on the three week tour, of 8,500 miles, visiting France, Italy, Greece, Yugoslavia, Malta, Gibraltar and Portugal. (RI–2911)

Air Marshal Sir George Mills meets crews from RAF Scampton who took part in a goodwill tour of Europe in 1954. (RI–2331)

Former 617 Squadron officers from the Royal Canadian Air Force looking at Lancaster 'S for Sugar' during their visit to RAF Scampton in 1959. (RI–2912)

An Avro Vulcan and a Lancaster lined up for an open day at RAF Scampton in 1959. (RI–3032)

A flypast by seven English Electric Canberra bombers at RAF Scampton, in 1953. (RI–955)

Sprucing up a Canberra bomber at RAF Scampton prior to At Home Day in 1953. (RI–942)

The casing of a 'bouncing bomb', the mine invented by Barnes Wallis, for 617 Squadron raids on the Ruhr Dams, being unloaded at RAF Scampton, in 1975, for display with the gate-guardian Lancaster. (75–Z–66)

High above the clouds, a Handley-Page Hastings of 1066 Squadron, at RAF Scampton in 1977. (77–42–E)

An impressive picture of two of A.V. Roe and Co. Ltd's most famous aircraft. The Lancaster flies over on line up of Vulcans. Both types of planes served with 617 The Dam Busters Squadron at RAF Scampton. (RI–964)

In the first half of the 1970s, RAF Scampton had both Hastings and Vulcans in service. Before the Hastings was withdrawn, both planes held an above the clouds rendezvous to enable photographs to be taken. (77–42–E)

Wing Commander Roger Maw was the creator of the wooden horse, which was used at a German Prison Camp to help prisoners escape. He visited RAF Scampton in 1975 to look at the Vulcan and Lancaster. (RI–2339)

'S for Sugar' on gate duty at RAF Scampton in 1959. The plane was eventually moved to the RAF Museum at Hendon. Its number was R5868 and it served with 83 Squadron as OL-Q (Queenie) and 467 Squadron as PO-S (Sugar). (RI–3467)

Crew run from their crew-coach to a waiting Avro Vulcan, in all white colouration, for a 'scramble' at RAF Scampton in August 1960. (RI–2184/5)

The Fairey Barracuda was a Naval Torpedo Bomber and was one of the aircraft used in attacks on the German battleship Tirpitz. *This aircraft was making an appearance at RAF Scampton in 1948, where it was being refuelled. (RI–734)*

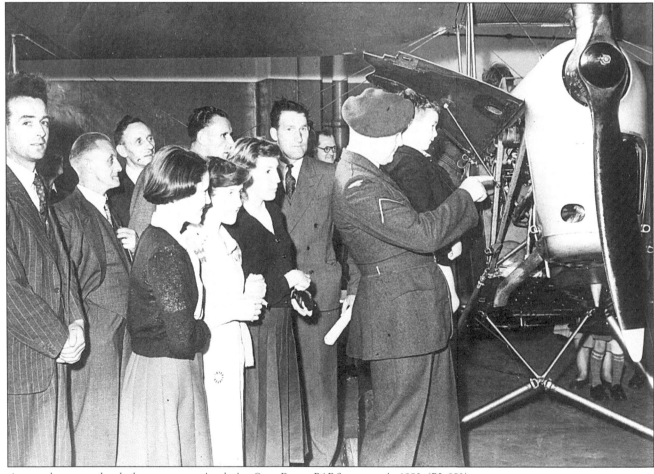

A young boy gets a close look at an aero engine during Open Day at RAF Scampton, in 1953. (RI–953)

Red trails in the sunset. The Red Arrows flying British Aerospace Hawks, when this picture was taken at RAF Scampton, leave a spectacular pattern of smoke as they fly into the sunset.

Musician Count Basie being welcomed to RAF Scampton for a concert in 1963. (RI–2880)

Nora Cooke's Memories

Nora Cooke, in the days when she was Nora Mitchell, in the Women's Auxiliary Air Force.

Nora Cooke has memories of Lancaster bombers. This one, 'S for Sugar', was gate guardian at RAF Scampton for many years.

Nora Cooke (née Mitchell) has memories of her time at RAF Scampton during the war years. She was a Sergeant in the Women's Auxiliary Air Force (WAAF) and now lives in Cleethorpes.

I gained an insight into the Dam Busters mission through working in the equipment section at RAF Scampton.

Things were ordered through the equipment section, so we knew what was coming into the base and what was going out.

In 1943, as the raid became imminent, we realised that it was an important mission, but still did not know what it was. It was all very hush-hush.

As the aircraft took off, they were flying very low because of the weight of the bombs they were carrying.

We wondered, as we did on all missions, of how many aircrew and aircraft would return.

It's quite awe-inspiring thinking about it today. After every mission, there would be people missing from the next function on the base.

People say that the raids on the dams were a waste of time and of no use, but that annoys me.

The raids did a lot of harm to Hitler and the pilots who flew on them were incredibly brave.

I still keep in touch with some of the women who lived on the base and when we get together, we talk fondly about our days at Scampton, when I was known by my nickname 'Micky Mitchell'.

We used to hitch-hike up to Cleethorpes at the weekends and go dancing on the pier, before we hitch-hiked back to Scampton.

The days I spent at the base during the war were the best days of my life. It was wonderful watching people working on the aircraft and I will never forget the noise of the engines.

I hope that now that the Red Arrows have arrived back at RAF Scampton, it will keep alive the memory of the brave pilots and crews of 617 Squadron.

RAF College, Cranwell

In 1915, the Admiralty requisitioned almost 3,000 acres of farmland near to the village of Cranwell and on 1 April 1916, the Royal Naval Air Station Cranwell opened.

It was known as HMS *Daedalus* and being technically a naval base, had a 'lighthouse', which is still kept today in the form of a flashing white beacon, on top of the college tower.

Two years after opening, Cranwell became RAF Cranwell, with the formation of the Royal Air Force from the amalgamation of the Royal Naval Air Service and the Royal Flying Corps.

Flying training continued at Cranwell until the end of 1919 and a Wireless School was also started.

Cranwell had its first royal visit in 1916, with King George V and Queen Mary being the visitors. Their second son, Prince Albert, later to become King George VI, was already a Naval Officer, but in 1918, he transferred to the Royal Air Force for a short time.

From 1920 to 1939, more than 1,100 flight cadets were trained at the base, which had now become the RAF Training College.

Many famous pilots trained at the college. One of the first to achieve fame was Flying Officer Henry Waghorn, AFC, winner of the Schneider Trophy in 1929. In 1930, under officer Douglas Bader graduated and became a legend in his own lifetime.

Cranwell became closely associated with long-distance flying in the late 1920s and '30s with the first non-stop flight to India taking place in 1929. Four years later, the first non-stop flight to South Africa was achieved.

One of the most famous flights ever to take place at Cranwell came in 1941, when the first jet-powered aircraft to fly in the United Kingdom took off. It was the Gloster Whittle E28/39, named after its inventor, Sir Frank Whittle, who was an apprentice at the college from 1923 to 1926, in the Boys' Wing and a flight cadet from 1926 to 1928. Sir Frank was the first Cranwell flight cadet to receive a knighthood.

The college closed on the outbreak of World War II and became the base for a number of flying training schools. After the war, it re-opened as a college in 1946.

In 1948, RAF College, Cranwell, had the distinction of becoming the recipient of the first Royal Air Force Colour ever awarded and this was paraded until 1960, when a new colour was presented by Queen Elizabeth II, to be followed another in 1975 and a fourth in 1989.

Many branches of the Air Force transferred to Cranwell. The Central Flying School transferred from RAF Scampton, in 1995, when that base closed and Cranwell became the home of the world famous Red Arrows. They moved back to Scampton in December 2000. The HQ Air Cadets moved from RAF Newton to RAF Cranwell in 1995 and absorbed HQ University Air Squadrons to form HQ University and Air Cadets.

Prince Charles with the Duke of Edingburgh, after the prince received his 'wings' at RAF College Cranwell. (RI–842)

Chief of the Air Staff in 1971, Air Chief Marshal Sir Denis Spotswood, presents 'wings' to Prince Charles at a Passing Out Parade at RAF College, Cranwell. (RI–842)

RAF College, Cranwell and Lords Taverners cricket teams who held a charity game in 1971. Prince Charles, playing for the college team, is seated fourth from left. (71/N–908)

Prince Charles takes to the field during the cricket match against the Lords Taverners. (71/N–980)

A helicopter carries a Land Rover and trailer. The transport aircraft are Blackburn Beverley (right) and Armstrong Whitworth Argosy. (RI–3150)

Troops abseil from helicopters at Unison '65. (RI–3150)

A pair of de Havilland Sea Vixens with their missile armament. These aircraft were the first British service fighters to dispense with gun armament. (RI–3150)

Paratroopers drop from an Armstrong Whitworth Argosy at Unison '65. (RI–3150)

Helicopters fly in to give support to the ground troops. (RI–3150)

The Blackburn Buccaneer, flown by the Royal Navy, has a large tail cone which opens into air brakes. (RI–3150)

The Handley Page Victor, with stand-off missile, at Unison '65. (RI–3150)

The Blackburn Beverley, at Unison '65. This aircraft could be used just as a troop carrier, or carry freight in its fuselage and a smaller number of troops in the tail-boom. (RI–3150)

Making what was possibly their first appearance in Lincolnshire, in 1965, the RAF Aerobatic Team, the Red Arrows, flying Folland Gnats, gave an impressive display at Unison '65. RAF Cranwell became the home of the Red Arrows from 1996 until RAF Scampton re-opened in 2000. (RI 3150)

Forerunner of the Harrier, the P1127 hovers at RAF Cranwell, in 1965, with an Avro Andover on the runway. (RI–3150)

Creating a cloud of spray and dust, the P1127 lands at RAF Cranwell, during Unison '65. It later became the Harrier, capable of vertical take-off and landing. (RI–3150)

Some of the service chiefs from Commonwealth countries at Unison '65. (RI–3150)

RAF College, Cranwell surrounded by scaffolding in November 1950. On top of the tower is a revolving white light indicating its origin as a Naval Air Service station. (RI–419)

Douglas Bader is the centre figure of this painting which was presented to RAF College, Cranwell. (RI–825)

Group Capt Douglas Bader (left) at RAF College, Cranwell, in July 1950 when the painting was presented to the college. (RI–825)

RAF Cranwell became a film set in 1957 when Warwick Productions made the film High Flight, *a story of the RAF in peacetime. Director of photography Ted Moore (wearing hat) makes a check before the cameras roll. (RI–3466)*

Among the stars taking part in the film were Kenneth Haigh, Jan Holden and Ray Milland. (RI–3466)

Joy Cooper's Memories

Joy Cooper in her Royal Observer Corps uniform.

Joy Cooper lived in Lincoln throughout World War II and now lives in Devon. Her memories are recorded in a booklet *My War, 1934-1945* and these are some of her recollections, especially about the time when she served in the Royal Observer Corps.

By 1942, there were lots of planes in the air, day and night and Lincoln High Street became a sea of Air Force blue – the county being home to many

Joy Cooper at her home in Devon.

operational airfields with their crews.

At the large Methodist church which had been my 'second home' since I was a blonde little girl of four years of age in the Sunday School and later a teacher and member of the large choir along with my mother, we kept on singing.

On Sunday evenings, after the service, we young folk put on a social and refreshments for the many servicemen and women who were there – these changed from week to week as they were posted to other areas or more sadly were killed on 'Ops'. We met some wonderful people and talented ones too – a little Army private would turn out to be a good singer, or a violinist, or a pianist. The talent was there and we enjoyed having our many and varied guests from the Forces and often invited them to our homes the following week.

I'm thinking now of one of our regulars – a little Scotsman in RAF uniform who stayed at Scampton for nearly four years, servicing the bombers as part of the ground crew. He was called Hamilton Mairs, otherwise 'Hammy', often a guest in our home being a lively cheerful young Christian.

In early 1943, 'Hammy' was sent to Canada for training as a 'tail-end Charlie', otherwise a rear gunner and was thrilled that he was going to be aircrew. After almost a year, he came back, went on his first 'Op' and was killed when the plane crash-landed. We were all so upset at losing our dear little

'Hammy' – he had been part of the family and would have been about 22 or maybe 23 years old.

I joined the Royal Observer Corps and in April, 1943, was transferred to the ROC headquarters in St Martin's Hall, in the centre of Lincoln.

I was very proud to be wearing the blue ROC uniform, very similar to that of the Women's Auxiliary Air Force and a 'Chipbag' hat, which later on was changed for a beret. It was all very 'hush-hush' and exciting and we new girls had to sign a secrecy document to tell no one – not even our parents, what happened inside that building.

We had two to three weeks training on the plotting table – virtually a map of Lincolnshire and a dozen girls wearing head phones sat around the table, each plotter being connected to three or four posts out in the country manned by locals, farmers, tradesmen, teachers, whatever, who had their own work to do first but manned each post around the clock. I admired these men very much, they were really dedicated to their job and learned to know by ear if the planes overhead were friendly, or hostile.

They gave us the height, type of plane and its direction and we put down our counters which plotted its course on the table. The counters were coloured and we had to put down the same colours as the clock was showing – red, blue or yellow.

On a balcony above and looking down were the tellers

Royal Observer Corps members around a plotting table. (RI–3409)

who could see the whole picture and relay it to Digby Centre, where the RAF took over the situation and decide whether to send out their planes when hostile ones were in the area.

We had quite a lot of activity and I remember the Dam Busters speeding over to bomb the dams in Germany, though we were never told any details – only plotted them!

We had one day off in three weeks, an exhausting schedule. We took sandwiches for our 'dinner', whenever that shift occurred, sometimes at midnight and on quiet shifts we had a few laughs and merry banter with our posts.

During my time in the Royal Observer Corps, a group of plotters, including myself, were sent on a course to the Operations Room at RAF Digby fighter station. To us, it was like being on holiday as we were billeted in a large manor house, Metheringham Hall and had a relaxed and enjoyable

week there, living and working with the WAAF Plotters.

We envied their comparatively easy life of regular hours on duty each day; lots of free time and teabreaks. Their food in the canteen was of the very best and lots of it! Oh yes, how I wish I'd volunteered to be a WAAF! But I would probably have been sent to the Outer Hebrides, as it was the Government's policy to send recruits as far away as possible from their homes, probably very wise as one then couldn't slip home quickly for a bit of home cooking and a hug from mum.

From early 1943 until the end of the war in Europe, in 1945, the skies over Lincolnshire were filled in the evenings with the sound of heavy bombers, mainly Lancasters, circling around higher and higher for a long time until finally they flew off to join the thousand bombing raids on Germany which finally brought defeat to Hitler and his Nazi regime.

As someone remarked – 'We counted them out and we counted them back' in the early hours of the morning, praying that those brave young men were safely back from yet another hazardous mission, but of course many were lost, shot down over Germany.

I enjoyed my time in the ROC at Lincoln Centre and felt that I was doing my bit for the war effort. I stayed in for 15 months and just in time to plot all the planes going south in readiness for the Second Front and the Normandy landings, then on 5 June 1944, I fainted at my post from sheer exhaustion, lack of sleep and food. So to my great disappointment, my doctor would not let me return to ROC duties and I was sent to the Council Offices and a desk job. Deadly dull, but regular hours for meals and sleeptime and I soon recovered.

I was disappointed to be left out of the Victory Parade at the end of the war, but – that's life!

VIP Visitors

There can hardly be a week in the life of an RAF station without a visit by someone, and the more important of these visits are recorded by the local press.

In this section of *Big Skies Over Lincolnshire*, photographs of some these VIP visits are featured.

There are many occasions when members of the royal family visit RAF stations and these are usually on anniversaries, special parades or to present squadrons with their Standards.

But it is not only royal visits which are featured. Over the years, there have been many times when the visitor was a high-ranking officer from an allied force, or former members of the Royal Air Force, now well-known names throughout the world, who have returned to the bases on which they served.

Accompanied by the Commandant of RAF College, Cranwell, the Queen and the Duke of Edingburgh, arrive at the college in 1970, the 50th anniversary of its opening. (L–17)

The College Colour is paraded at the celebrations. (L–17)

College Officer Cadets on parade at the 50th anniversary celebrations. (L–17)

The Queen, accompanied by Air Vice-Marshal Desmond Hughes, Commandant of RAF College Cranwell, meets local schoolchildren at RAF College, Cranwell. (L–17)

A Sopwith Snipe, built by Ruston's, in Lincoln, during World War I, formed part of the static display at RAF College Cranwell. (L–17)

A special day at RAF Scampton, in August 1963, when General Lyman L. Lemnitzer, Supreme Allied Commander in Europe visited the base. (RI–2533)

General Lemnitzer inspects a guard of honour formed by members of the RAF Regiment. (RI–2533)

General Lemnitzer is driven past an Avro Vulcan during his visit. (RI–2534)

Canberra bombers lined up for the General's inspection. (RI–2534)

Vickers Valiant bombers, part of the RAF's 'V' force are inspected by General Lemnitzer. (RI–2534)

The Queen visited RAF Scampton in June 1963 to present a Standard to 83 Squadron which had just completed 25 years continuous service. Saluting the Queen is the station's Commanding Officer, Group Captain K.G. Hubbard and second from right is Air-Vice Marshal Patrick Dunn, Air Officer Commanding No 1 Group Bomber Command. (RI–2464)

The Queen presents a Standard to 83 Squadron Standard Bearer, Flying Officer R.M. Ward, in June 1963. (RI–2464)

Air Commodore Sir Frank Whittle returned to RAF College, Cranwell to open a new instructional block in 1962. (RI–852)

Sir Frank Whittle takes a nostalgic look at the Whittle W1 gas turbine engine of the type which powered the Gloster E28/39 aircraft and made the first jet powered flight at RAF Cranwell on 15 May 1941. The engine was developed into the Derwent, which was used to power the Gloster Meteor. (RI–852)

Princess Mary, the Princess Royal, in 1964, visited RAF Hospital Nocton Hall on a day when umbrellas were very much in evidence. (RI–2325)

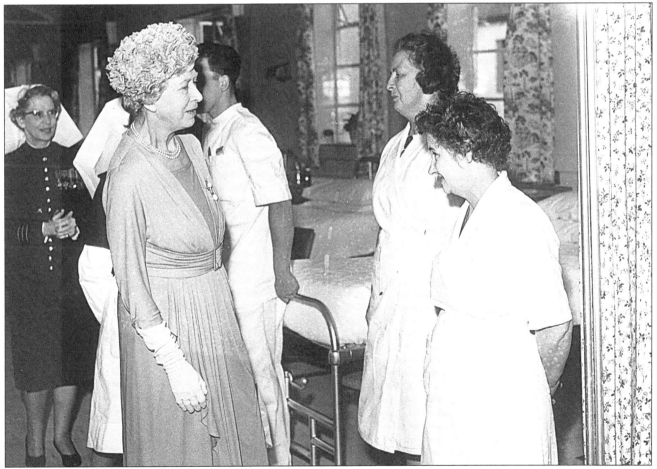

The Princess Royal meets staff at the hospital. (RI–2326)

Princess Marina, Duchess of Kent, inspects members of 44 and 50 Squadrons at RAF Waddington, in 1967, when she presented Standards to them. (RI–2475)

Chief of Staff of the USAF, General Thomas D. White, arrived at RAF Waddington in September 1958 and during his visit, inspected a guard of honour. (RI–3994)

A Standard is paraded at RAF Waddington in 1967. Standards were presented by the Duchess of Kent to both 44 and 50 Squadrons. (RI–2476)

Prince Philip carries out an inspection at a Passing-out-Parade in 1953. (RI–842)

The Duke of Edingburgh arrives at RAF College, Cranwell for a Passing-out-Parade in July 1953. (RI 842)

Major General William Blanchard, of the United States Air Force meets Vulcan crews at RAF Waddington in September 1957. (RI–2191)

The Boeing B-47 Stratojet which brought Major General Blanchard to RAF Waddington framed by one of the station's Vulcan bombers. (RI–2191)

In 1948 King George VI, accompanied by Queen Elizabeth and Princess Margaret, visited RAF College Cranwell to present the first King's Colour to be granted within the RAF. (RI–415)

Queen Elizabeth, now the Queen Mother, arrives at RAF College, Cranwell, in 1948. (RI–415)

King George VI inspects cadets at RAF Cranwell in 1948. (RI–415)

Royal Canadian Air Force officers meet the Queen Mother during her visit to RAF Scampton in 1959. (RI–2328)

A proud moment for members of 617 Squadron as they are inspected by the Queen Mother in 1959. (RI–2329)

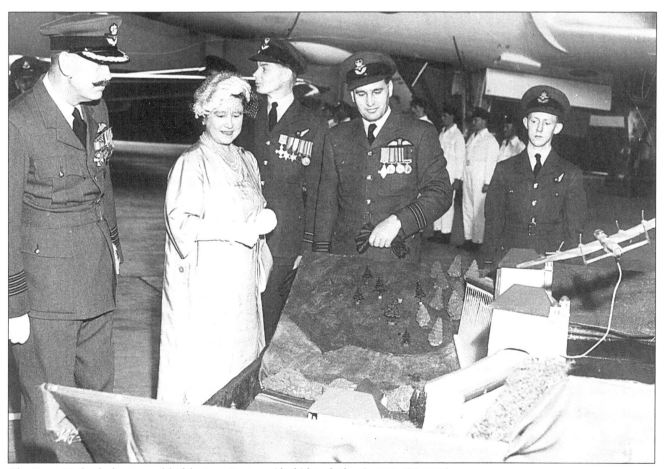

The Queen Mother looks at a model of the Dam Busters raid which took place in 1943. (RI–2119)

Queen Elizabeth, the Queen Mother, visited RAF Scampton in 1959 to present a Standard to 617 Squadron. The Queen Mother carried out an inspection of squadron members. (RI–2119)

The crew of a Vulcan bomber meet the Queen Mother during her visit to RAF Scampton, in 1959. (RI–2329)

Pictured at RAF Scampton in 1959, when the Queen Mother visited the base, the only other flying Lancaster, from Canada. (Bill Baker Collection)

Rex Wheeldon's Memories

Squadron Leader (retired) Rex Wheeldon.

Retired Squadron Leader Rex Wheeldon served with the Royal Air Force for 30 years and many of his postings were at Lincolnshire bases. He now lives at Buslingthorpe and is Central Committee Chairman of the Wickenby Register.

I first came into Lincolnshire in connection with the Air Force in 1936. I failed to qualify for a short service commission in 1935, but found that with Trenchard's expansion, they had decided to enlist direct entry pilots. I thought this was my chance so I applied for a entry as a direct entry sergeant pilot and was accepted and started my flying training in 1936 and in March was posted to 3 Flying Training School at Grantham, nowadays called Spitalgate and there, having learned to fly on Tiger Moths, we were then presented with Avro Tutors, Hawker Harts and Audaxes.

The Hart was converted to a two-seater trainer in which we learned how to handle these aeroplanes, which we did and eventually I left Grantham on posting to 207 squadron, at Worthy Down, just outside Winchester. The squadron had just returned from the Eritrean frontier when the Abyssinian troubles were on the go.

I found myself in a world which was quite unknown, to them and to me. I'd never had anything to do with the services before and the services had never seen Direct Entry Sergeants before, but we got on alright together.

My squadron was equipped with Fairey Gordon aircraft which were of 1922 vintage, an open-cockpit biplane, cruising at about 90 mph. On exercises, we had to climb up to about 14,000 feet, so we had to smear our faces with anti-frost grease, we wrapped ourselves up as well as we could, balaclavas around our heads underneath our helmets, big goggles covering most of our face, silk scarves, silk gloves, woollen gloves, leather gloves, wool suits underneath our sidcot suits and fur lined boots.

And it was still cold at 14,000 feet, temperatures would get down to about minus 40.

That went on until they decided that the Air Force wanted new types of aeroplanes and we were given the new long-range monoplane, the Vickers Wellesley, it had made a name for itself, by running the long distance record from Egypt to India, non-stop.

We kept those for some time, moving from Worthy Down, up to Cottesmore in Rutland, which had just opened up. We lived in wooden huts and we did quite a lot of development flying on the Wellesleys, going for quite long distances.

We found a strange thing after flying for a long time, the

Leading Aircraftman Rex Wheeldon at 3 Flying Training School, Grantham, in 1936.

Wellesley had six fuel tanks, three in each wing, and for some extraordinary reason, which they believed was from the backwash of the propellor of the aircraft, the fuel would drain out of one set of tanks, and the other fuel tanks would not drain into the collector box at the bottom, which meant that you had an aeroplane with one heavy wing and one empty wing, the result of which, unfortunately, caused a pilot friend of mine to lose his life when he crashed at Upper Heyford as he couldn't keep the aircraft in the air any longer.

They discovered that the problem was the air venting of the fuel tanks, so they took the air vents on the six tanks up into the wireless mast behind the cockpit. Once they were positioned there, it cured the trouble.

Then they decided that the Wellesley was an aeroplane which should be used in the Middle East, so we lost our Wellesleys and took on the new Fairey Battle, which was a marvellous aeroplane, from the point of view of the fact that we were not at war, but once we got to war, it was not what it ought to be.

When the war started, I had what was called a war appointment and I went down to Andover where they were forming a communications squadron to work with the BEF when it went into France and I flew to war in a Tiger Moth. I was one of the early ones to go across and I had to fly from Shoreham to Le Treport on my way down to a place called Laval.

Rex Wheeldon, then a Flight Sergeant, with his crew at RAF Binbrook in 1941.

It was a bit of a novelty, because we didn't quite know what we were supposed to be doing and we were told that we should fire a recognition light when we got to Le Treport, which I did, and expected to see some sort of response. There was none, so having circled the place a couple of times, I carried on to Laval.

I was attached to 50 Wing and the Commanding Officer was a very famous officer, Wing Cmdr Ferdinand Maurice Felix West, VC, MC. He had been flying in World War I, a shell knocked one of his legs off and he managed to finish the job he was doing and get the aeroplane back on the ground, for which he got his VC.

After that, when the Germans became active, we were sent back to refresh our memories on how to fly the Fairey Battle and I was posted to join 12 Squadron, after the infamous raid on the Maastricht bridges, when we lost so many of our aircraft.

We were supposed after that not to be doing daylight raids, but I was in France flying both day and night-time operations. There were no mass raids at all, we all went off individually to find our target, whatever it was, and drop our bombs on them. A lot of times, we couldn't identify targets and took our bombs back home. On two occasions we were out in daylight, and got picked up by a German fighter. The first time, my gunner at the back saw the German starting to dive on me and warned me so I looked up, saw him coming down and turned in underneath him, because we had been told that the ME109 pilots didn't like to get into too steep a dive because they had problems pulling out again.

So I turned in under him, and sure enough, he flew out over the top of me, I saw him fire his cannon because I saw a streak of dirty black smoke and he disappeared into the blue and we went on our way. The second attack, the enemy came up from underneath my tailplane and of course my gunner didn't see him coming. The next thing I knew, there was a funny sound from out on the left wing and when I looked out to the left, there were a lot of bright lights shooting forwards from the end of the wing. As I realised what was happening, this ME109 went over the top of us about 20 feet away. There was one front gun in the Battle, but I was flying along with the button on 'safe'. By the time I had thought about turning it on to 'fire', he had disappeared into the blue but he had blown all the covering off my left aileron so I had to fly back home keeping the control column over to the right in order to keep the aeroplane on a level keel.

Later, France collapsed but we were still there for a month after the Dunkirk evacuation although we got out the day before the capitulation and ended up landing in Shoreham. It was rather nice to be back home again. On the way in, the boys at the nearby Lancing College could be seen playing cricket and the sight of that compared with what we had left behind was something I shall never forget.

We were then sent to Finningley and from there, became one of the two squadrons which moved in to the newly opened RAF Binbrook. We flew from there in our Fairey Battles, chiefly on night operations bombing ports in France where the Geman invasion barges were assembling. We had one or two occasions when intruders came over which made life a little bit difficult. We also had a few attacks on the airfield, for-tunately, nothing very serious. Once they dropped a load of incendiary bombs but before they had got high enough to drop heavier bombs, the

incendiaries were extinguished and when the bombs came down, they fell in the fields near the airfield and not on it.

Our aircraft were changed and we were given the MkII Wellingtons. That was a great improvement which meant you could then fly at 16 or 17 thousand feet, which was two or three thousand feet higher than the Mk I's,

We went to briefings to find out what the target was, but each aircraft was an individual effort. Our navigators did all the work to tell us where to go and we went off at intervals, seldom seeing anybody else. On one occasion, I remember we went over to Bremen, in June, and in the middle of the year, you had the Northern Lights giving a great white glow in the sky, to the north; to the south, we a had full moon. We were stuck between the two as we flew across to Bremerhaven then down into Bremen and all the way down, ahead of us, you could see something going on, flashes in the sky, and I distinctly remember seeing a string of dotted lights which was obviously somebody firing a canon with incendiary shells, following which there was an explosion and three lumps of something burning went floating down to the ground – an aircraft which had been shot down.

We had a fairly heavy load flying at 16 or 17 thousand feet and as bombs went off and the load was released, the nose of the aeroplane went up and we ended up at 22,000 feet.

On another earlier raid on Duisberg, we found on returning home that at that greater height, there were different winds and we ran into a stronger head wind than we expected. When we finally got to the French coastline, we were getting a bit short on fuel but we made it back to England, landed on a 'Darkie' call at Honington, refuelled and continued back to Lincolnshire.

Binbrook was an interesting place because on more than one occasion when there was a north easterly wind, we would be briefed for an operation, but by the time we came to take off, a north sea 'haar' had rolled in and it blotted out the airfield.

Having been taken off operational flying because of ear trouble, I was posted to RAF Scampton to join No 1518 Beam Approach Training Flight. We found ourselves working in a hangar, half of which belonged to 617 Squadron. It was a fairly big building but there was a sheet hanging across the middle of the hangar, it was the biggest sheet I have ever seen. On the other side, 617 Squadron aircraft were being prepared for their specialised trip bombing the dams. You were under pain of death to go the other side of that sheet, so we didn't!

I had one small hand in the bombing of the dams. I was asked to take an armament Flight Lieutenant to North Coates. He was going to pick something up. It turned out to be mine fuses for the 'bouncing bombs'. After that, training

The Fairey Battle, one of the types of aircraft flown by Rex Wheeldon.

aircraft were taken out of Lincolnshire and I was posted with the flight to Scotland.

After my time as an instructor on Beam Approach was up, I was given the option of doing calibration of these radio landing beams and went to airfields all over the UK. We were then flying Anson aircraft and our job was to go round all the fields where these aids were fitted to make sure they were in 'good nick'.

In 1962, I was posted to RAF Waddington at the time when the Vulcan was being introduced. I had been sent off after the war to do a course as an accounting officer and became Squadron Leader (Accounts) at Waddington when they were introducing the Vulcan.

From Waddington, I was sent down to Fighter Command where I was working on 'Establishments', which meant that every so often, I had a trip out to one of the fighter stations to examine the establishment of the unit to find out if we could 'pinch' any of the people and put them somewhere else. After that, Fighter Command had opened up in Binbrook and they wanted someone to come up to that station as Squadron Leader (Admin) and as I lived in Lincolnshire, they thought I was the right person to take up the post at Binbrook, which I did in June 1965 and stayed there until I retired in December 1966.

Big Events

From time to time, there have been events at Lincolnshire RAF stations which have been of national importance.

Our photographs show some of these.

During 1964, RAF Coningsby was closed for a complete refurbishment and to mark the occasion, exercised their right, as holders of the Freedom of the Borough of Boston, to march through the town.

In 1965, Unison '65, was the name given to a special display at RAF College, Cranwell, at the end of a special conference attended by service chiefs from all branches of the armed forces throughout the Commonwealth.

Displays were given by the Royal Navy, the Army and the Royal Air Force to show how air power is used by these services.

It was also the first season for the Royal Air Force's Aerobatic Display Team, the Red Arrows and their display brought the event to a close, an event which had also seen a display by the forerunner of the Harrier vertical take-off aircraft. In order to make the chapters of this book more equal in length, this event has been included in the RAF Cranwell section.

Some other events have also been included in the section appropriate to their location.

In 1968, Bomber Command was disbanded and together with Fighter Command, was reformed into Strike Command. The Stand Down of Bomber Command was held at RAF Scampton, an occasion of great nostalgia for many. Included among the many guests present were Marshal of the Royal Air Force Sir Arthur 'Bomber' Harris, Group Capt Leonard Cheshire, VC, Barnes Wallis, (knighted during this year), and Denis Healey, then Minister of Defence.

There was also a major event in the county during 1976, when the Battle of Britain Memorial flight was relocated in the county at RAF Coningsby.

An event from 1984 saw the end of service for the Avro Vulcan bomber. This aircraft had been a familiar sight in the skies over Lincolnshire for three decades. One aircraft was kept in flying condition for a few years before it made its farewell flight over the county. It is now preserved at an air museum but there are hopes and a campaign to get it back into the air once again.

Mayor of Boston in 1964, Coun. Bert Eyre, inspects contingents from RAF Coningsby at a farewell parade in the town. (RI 3066)

Standard parties from 9, 12 and 35 Squadrons at RAF Coningsby on parade at Boston, before the base was closed for refurbishment. (RI–3036)

RAF Coningsby has the Freedom of the Borough of Boston and exercised their rights to march with fixed bayonets and colours flying on their 'farewell' parade. (RI–3036)

Denis Healey meets ground crew during the Stand Down of Bomber Command, in 1968, at RAF Scampton. (RI–2452)

Denis Healey talks to ground crew at the Stand Down against a background of a vintage biplane and Vulcan Bombers. (RI–2542)

Marshal of the Royal Air Force, Sir Arthur Harris (fourth from left) wartime head of Bomber Command, at the Stand Down. (RI–2542)

'Bomber' Harris no doubt found much to remind him of his time as Chief of Bomber Command, at the Stand Down. (RI–2542)

Denis Healey inspects air and ground crew at the Stand Down. (RI–2542)

One of many inspections being carried out at the Stand Down. (RI–2540)

Back at his former base, Group Captain Leonard Cheshire (right) who was awarded the Victoria Cross in World War II. (RI–2540)

Group Captain Leonard Cheshire (centre) was awarded the Victoria Cross for the number of operations (100) he carried out, rather than for any one act of courage. He served in 617 Squadron at both Coningsby and Woodhall Spa. He was the British observer of the second A-bomb attack, on Nagasaki. Group Captain Cheshire founded the Cheshire Foundation Home for incurably sick and received a peerage in 1991, taking the title Baron Cheshire of Woodhall. (RI–2542)

Among the guests at RAF Scampton in 1968 was Barnes Wallis (left) inventor of the 'Bouncing Bomb', used by 617 The Dam Busters squadron who flew from Scampton in 1943. (RI–2540)

Denis Healey meets more of the crews at RAF Scampton during the Stand Down ceremony. (RI–2540)

Third from left on the front row of this group is Denis Healey (now Lord Healey) who was Defence Minister in 1968. Third from right on the row is Marshal of the Royal Air Force, Sir Arthur Harris, 'Bomber Harris' who was in command of Bomber Command in World War II. (RI–2540)

The Red Arrows performing at the Stand Down. (RI–2540)

A Handley Page Victor tanker re-fuelling an English Electric Lightning at the Stand Down of Bomber Command. (RI–2540)

Two Avro Vulcans give a display at the Stand Down. (RI–2540)

Although the Handley Page Victor was often used as a re-fuelling tanker, its original role was as a bomber and in 1968, at the Stand Down of Bomber Command, one flew with an Avro Blue Steel stand off nuclear missile slung beneath its fuselage. (RI–2540)

Mayor of Lincoln, Alderman Sidney (Jock) Campbell was among the guests at the Stand Down. (RI–2540)

The City of Lincoln 'adopted' the RAF's last flying Lancaster in 1974 with the Mayor of Lincoln, Councillor Tom Ward taking part in the ceremony. (74–2–560)

Symmetry in the air from the Red Arrows at the 'adoption' of the City of Lincoln Lancaster, at RAF Waddington in 1974. (74–2–560)

Mayor of Lincoln in 1976 Councillor Fred Allen, meets the crew of the Lancaster which was adopted by the City of Lincoln. (76–3–3–B)

Left to right: Spitfire Mk XIX representing an aircraft of No.11 Squadron and Hurricane Mk IIC with code LE-D, to commemorate the aircraft flown by Squadron Leader Douglas Bader. The Lancaster with the code KM-B, is in markings to commemorate the aircraft in which Squadron Leader John Nettleton flew when awarded the Victoria Cross. (76–3–3–B)

The Battle of Britain Memorial Flight at their new home, RAF Coningsby, in March 1976. (76–3–3–B)

Dakota ZA947, with the Lancaster and Spitfire Mk XIX. (76–3–3–B)

Squadron Leader Douglas Bader flew with 242 (Canadian) Squadron, based at Coltishall and Duxford, during the Battle of Britain. Hurricane Mk IIC carries the letters LE-D to commemorate this legendary pilot. (76–3–3–B)

A Spitfire Mk IIA UO-T (left) and Spitfire Mk XIX. PS915 in plain blue colour, the standard scheme for RAF photographic reconnaissance aircraft. (76–3–3–B)

Spitfire PS915, a Mk XIX in the blue colours of a photographic reconnaissance aircraft. (76–3–3–B)

With the word 'Farewell' painted on the inside of its bomb doors, the Vulcan makes its farewell flight over Lincoln after being retired from service in 1984.

The last Avro Vulcan flies over Lincoln Cathedral.

Peter Washbourn's Memories

Peter Washbourn

Living all my life in Lincoln, I had become used to seeing and hearing aeroplanes during World War II and after marriage, my wife Pat and I eventually went to live in a house over which Vulcans (and other aircraft) flew daily on their circuits around RAF Waddington.

But it was when I became a press photographer, in 1960, that my connections became frequent. I had failed the medical for National Service. Had I passed, I would have liked to 'get some in' with the RAF, hopefully in the photographic section.

I think my first visit to a Royal Air Force base was in 1959, before I became a press photographer, when I went to RAF Scampton on its open day.

RAF Scampton and RAF Waddington were the bases I visited most frequently, although I did visit RAF College Cranwell, Swinderby and Coningsby many times. Some weeks, a visit to an airbase was a daily occurrence. One week, I went to RAF Scampton on Monday and outside the guardroom were two airmen with a large tin of polish and very small brushes. They were polishing the tiles, over which everyone was still walking to get into the building. At the end of the week, on another visit, they were still there. Same brushes, but the tin of polish was almost empty. I don't know what they had done wrong but they certainly found out what 'jankers' meant that week!

Another time, I arrived at RAF Waddington for a function in their theatre, The Lancastria. I was told that I would need an escort and an airman was dispatched with me to the theatre. Outside the guard-room, he asked "Do you know where it is? I don't." So I escorted him!

I flew with the RAF four times. The first time was in a Hercules, during an exercise dropping members of the TA over Norfolk. What a big plane that was! I was allowed up on the flight deck during the return trip. I could not believe the space – I had, up till then, flown mostly in small two-seater private aircraft in very cramped conditions.

Another trip was in a Bulldog trainer. This was a very small aircraft but with plenty of room in the cockpit and excellent visibility for taking pictures. It was a bit alarming having to wear flying kit and parachute and the instruction from the pilot didn't help the nerves. "If I say jump, then jump and pull the ripcord!"

I was also taken up for a short flight in a helicopter to photograph, from the open doorway, a line of Phantom bombers on the runway at RAF Coningsby. "Don't drop you camera, we haven't got time to go looking for the bits!"

But the most memorable flight was in a Hastings. We took off from RAF Scampton for a rendezvous with a Vulcan, somewhere 'up north'. It was January and foggy, but above the fog, there was bright sunshine and we soon found our 'target' and a second Hastings. It was a very noisy flight. The doors and windows had been taken out of the fuselage of the Hastings, so that we could get good pictures without the bother of reflections in the glass.

For a quarter of an hour, we took pictures and at one time, we could see a perfectly circular rainbow on the clouds below us, with the shadow of our aircraft in its centre, a truly amazing sight.

Two particular events at RAF stations remain in my mind more than others.

Unison '65 was the name of a very big exercise at RAF Cranwell in 1965 and on the final day, the flying display was

Flight Lieutenant Joe 'Spike' Hughes, Press Relations Officer at RAF Waddington in the 1960s, accompanies members of the press at an event at RAF Waddington. Peter Washbourn, nearest camera, with Gerald Murray and Cyril Middleton (right). Picture by courtesy C.V. Middleton and Son.

the best I have ever seen. It was also the first time that I had seen the Red Arrows and it may have been their first visit to the county in their first season.

In 1968, Bomber Command was stood down and at the ceremony, there were many famous people present. Marshal of the Royal Air Force, Sir Arthur ('Bomber') Harris, Barnes Wallis, Group Capt Leonard Cheshire and Denis Healey, who was then the Minister of Defence.

I attended many royal visits to county RAF stations, including several at the time when Prince Charles was

training at RAF College, Cranwell.

But my favourite story is one which happened at RAF Scampton during a 'Good Neighbours' day.

A very prominent local dignitary, getting on a little in years, was invited to take a look around the cockpit of a Vulcan and I was also invited to go into the 'plane. It all went very well until the VIP tried to leave the cockpit, via the ladder which had extensions at the top, to hold on to until you got on to the step. He managed to get these extensions up his trouser leg, one each side and was well

and truly stuck. He had to be lifted off by two officers. Me, I pretended to be looking at some of the equipment in the cockpit. Well, I couldn't let them see my amused look. The only regret I have is that I wasn't allowed to take a camera with me, because of security.

There is one moment which will remain in my memory forever. On one graduation parade, at RAF College, Cranwell, I noticed a familiar looking figure walking stiff-legged across the parade ground. It was Group Capt Douglas Bader. I approached, introduced myself and asked if

I could take his photograph? "Of course, lad," he said "but don't take too long or this ruddy wind will blow me over." Absolute magic!

My last visit to an RAF base was to RAF Cranwell, in February 1996. The Red Arrows had been on a tour since the previous summer and were returning to Cranwell, which was to become their new home, after the closure of RAF Scampton. There was snow on the ground and we were waiting at the side of the runway for almost an hour, there had been a slight delay on their return. It was then that the full impact became apparent of a phrase I had heard many times about Lincolnshire air bases – 'Siberia with grass.' Never more true than on that day!

Group Captain Douglas Bader, on a windy day at RAF Cranwell.

Around Bomber County

Whilst it is correct to say that *Echo* photographers attended events at RAF Waddington, RAF Scampton and RAF College, Cranwell more frequently than at any other bases, there were occasions when they took photographs at other RAF stations in Lincolnshire.

RAF Coningsby, RAF Binbrook, RAF Hemswell and others all feature in this section of *Big Skies Over Lincolnshire* which shows some of the many types of aircraft which have flown over the county.

There are also pictures of some of the incidents when, unhappily, aircraft crashed, but fortunately there was no loss of life in these accidents.

This section is, therefore, one in which photographs which did not really fall into the categories of other sections have been included. It is varied and hopefully will bring back memories for many people.

Ground and support crew members pose for a photograph before 139 Squadron, at RAF Hemswell, in 1955, set off on a tour of Canada and Jamaica.

A last minute briefing before take off on the 21,000 miles tour to include the Canadian National Exhibition, in Toronto and Jamaica's Tercentenary celebrations. (RI–958)

Squadron Leader A. Ashworth, Commanding Officer of 139 Squadron and his navigator Flight-Lieutenant J.S. Lodden, board their Canberra for the flight. (RI–958)

A line up Canberra Jet Bombers of 139 (Jamaica) Squadron RAF Hemswell ready for their tour of Canada and Jamaica in 1955. (RI–958)

A 139 Squadron Canberra taxies past the control tower at RAF Hemswell to fly to Canada. (RI–3538)

A 139 Squadron Canberra departs for the tour. (RI–0958)

Families wave 'Bon Voyage' to the departing crews at RAF Hemswell. (RI–3538)

An English Electric Canberra is prepared for the Battle of Britain open day at RAF Hemswell in September 1955. (RI–3465)

Mayor of Lincoln in April 1975, Councillor Tom Ward, inspects new recruits to the Royal Air Force, at RAF Swinderby at their Passing-out-Parade after initial training. (Y–694)

Mayor of Lincoln in May 1973 Councillor Wilf Pixsley performs one of the last duties of his year of office as inspecting officer at a Passing-out-Parade at RAF Swinderby. (T–557)

A Vulcan bomber makes a low fly-past as Mayor of Lincoln in May 1973, Councillor Wilf Pixsley reviews the Passing-out-Parade of new recruits at RAF Swinderby. (T–557)

THOR Ballistic Missiles were on standby in Lincolnshire during the 'Cold War' until they were removed in 1963. (RI–2546)

A THOR Ballistic Missile is prepared to be 'shipped out' from RAF Hemswell, in 1963. (RI–2546)

A giant C-133 Cargo Master aircraft was used to take THOR missiles from RAF Hemswell in 1963. (RI–2546)

A Vampire from RAF Cranwell crashed in a potato field near Cammeringham in October 1960. The crew baled out and landed safely. (RI–3697)

Three thousand members of the Royal Observer Corps held their annual camp at RAF Binbrook, in 1961. Just a few are pictured at Group Headquarters, Fiskerton. (RI–214)

The plotting table at the Royal Observer Corps' Group Headquarters, at Fiskerton. (RI–265)

Boeing B-29 Superfortress aircraft were a familiar sight over Lincolnshire for many years. (RI–735)

RAF Kirton Lindsey played host to the Lincoln Aero Club for their 'Fly-in' in 1965. Young visitors take a look at a sticker from a 1964 rally on the fuselage of this private aircraft. (RI–962)

5 Squadron, based at RAF Binbrook in 1966, celebrated its 50th anniversary on a day which brought back memories for many. (RI–3048)

An impressive line up of English Electric Lightning aircraft at 5 Squadron's 50th anniversary in 1966. (RI–3048)

A wet day meant an indoor inspection for 5 Squadron at RAF
Binbrook. The reviewing officer was Air Marshal (retired) Sir
Aubrey Ellwood, Squadron Commander in 1932/33. (RI–3048)

Royal Flying Corps pilot, Wing Commander (retired) Reuben
Hollingsworth (left) and ex-Flight Sergeant Jack Hamilton, are
brought up to date by LAC Roy Sampson, as they look around the
cockpit of a Lightning at RAF Binbrook. (RI–3048)

The first McDonnell Douglas F4 Phantoms to enter service with the Royal Air Force arrived at RAF Coningsby in August 1968. They were brought in to replace the TSR-2 aircraft project which was cancelled after the first of four TSR-2's had flown 13 hours and 14 minutes flying time during 24 flights. (G–504)

USAF Boeing Superfortress aircraft were a familiar sight over Lincolnshire in October 1950. (RI–454)

In the skies above Lincolnshire in 1977, the Lancaster PA474, in 44 Squadron markings and Spitfire P7350, in the markings of 266 (Rhodesia) Squadron. (77–321)

A Vampire from RAF Swinderby made an emergency landing at the former RAF Skellingthorpe airfield when its engine failed in December 1958. Fuel supplies were brought in and the plane was able to take-off. It is believed that this was the last plane to use the former airfield, which is now part of the Birchwood Housing Estate. (RI–959)

A Meteor Jet Fighter, from RAF Manby crashed in a field near Metheringham in 1954. The crew baled out and landed safely nearby. (RI–1429)

RAF recruits preparing de Havilland Vampires for Battle of Britain Day in 1956. (RI–2167)

In 1937, a Hampden Bomber crashed on approach to RAF Scampton. The pilot, who received injuries, misjudged his landing path and struck the chimney of Aisthorpe House. The chimney stack crashed through the roof of the house, slightly injuring the occupant and his young daughter. The aircraft crashed on to the lawn. (RI–283)

The Hurricane and Spitfire fly low past a Hawker Hart, a fighter from between the wars. (RI–2540)

The Handley Page Hampden bomber was a familiar sight in Lincolnshire skies during the early part of World War II. This picture was taken in 1941. (RI–476)

Moving by road, the Avro 707A was a small delta winged jet aircraft which was a fore-runner of the Avro Vulcan bomber. It is being moved along the A15 at Bracebridge Heath, where Avro had a factory in 1953. (RI–954)

Against a background of an Avro Lancaster, a mechanic works on restoration at the heritage centre at East Kikby.

Visitors to the Lincolnshire Aviation Heritage Centre, look at the casing of one of Barnes Wallis' 'Bouncing Bombs'.

A Queen Mary trailer and other military vehicles form part of the display at East Kirkby.

The former control tower at the Lincolnshire Aviation Heritage Centre.

Lancaster NX611, in the colours of 57 Squadron as DX-C, on the starboard side with the emblem 'Just Jane' on the port side nose, previously stood at the gateway to RAF Scampton. It is now at the Lincolnshire Aviation Heritage Centre, East Kirkby.

Out on the runway and ready to roll, 'Just Jane' at East Kirkby.

Lined up for the enthusiasts at an open day including a Sopwith Pup, an Avro 504K, a Jet Provost, a Lockheed Shooting Star Meteor and English Electr

...ightning.

Silhouetted against a Lincolnshire sky, the Battle of Britain Memorial Flight.

Avro Big and small. The mighty Vulcan dwarfs an Avro 504, which had its debut in 1913.

Youngsters get a close look at a Percival Provost trainer at an open day.

Two of the three 'V' force aircraft, a Vickers Valiant flies over an Avro Vulcan.

The Avro Shackleton, designed for marine reconnaissance, as well as a bomber carried a crew of 10. (RI–278X)

Giant in the sky, a Blackburn Beverley, with fixed undercarriage, could carry a large load in its body, with personnel accommodated in the tail boom. (RI–2537)

Symbol of the Battle of Britain, the Spitfire was one of the two planes (the other being the Hurricane) which dominated the skies. (RI–2537)

A strange sight, the Fairey Gannet AEW3, a flying radar control centre which has folding wings, for storage on board ship and a large ventral dome carrying the radar equipment. (RI–278X)

A United States Air Force Lockheed Shooting Star. This type of aircraft entered service in 1945 and more than 5,000 of the various series were produced. (RI–278X)

Five de Havilland Vampires fly over RAF Swinderby for the last time in 1964. The Vampire was the second turbojet-powered fighter, but came too late for service in World War II. (RI–2341)

Crews of the last de Havilland Vampires to fly at RAF Swinderby, in 1964. (RI–2341)

A giant among aircraft, a C-130 Hercules is being used here as a personnel carrier.

The Battle of Britain Memorial Flight in close formation, with the City of Lincoln Lancaster flanked by Spitfire Mk XIX PM 631, which was used in the film The Battle of Britain *and Hurricane Mk IIC, LF363, which also appeared in the film, with a series of fictitious numbers.*

Battle of Britain Memorial Flight's Dakota III, served with the Royal Aircraft Establishment, later the Defence Research Agency before joining the flight. It is seen here in wartime camouflage to commemorate the 1944 airborne landings at Arnhem.

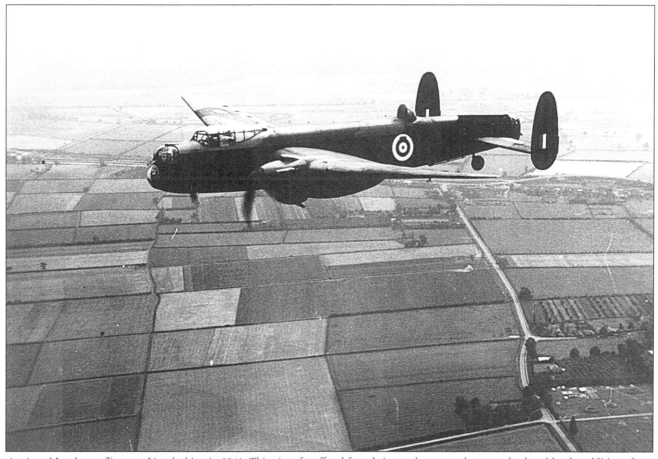

An Avro Manchester flies over Lincolnshire, in 1941. This aircraft suffered from being under-powered, so was developed by the addition of two more engines, into the Lancaster. (Bill Baker collection)

Lancaster PA474, a Mk 1, which was built just too late to see service in World War II. After storage, it was converted into a photo-reconnaissance aircraft. Lincolnshire became its home in 1965. (76–3–3–B)

The Lancaster was eventually developed into the Avro Lincoln and RF386 is pictured flying over the north of Lincoln. The Lincoln was replaced in RAF Service by the Canberra jet bomber. (RI–737)

The fourth development in the sequence Manchester – Lancaster – Lincoln, was the Avro Shackleton, first flown in 1949. It had four engines powering contra-rotating propellers and was used in both maritime reconnaissance and early warning roles. (278X)

The Manchester Bomber, powered by two Rolls-Royce Vulture engines, was under-powered, so it was decided to fit it with four Merlin engines. This Manchester III then became the prototype Lancaster. A Manchester was dumped in a gravel pit at Burton, in 1942 and used to practice escape drills. It was dismantled lifted and taken by road to Sturgate, in 1956, by the USAF to teach American airman how to escape from blazing wrecks. (RI–2467B)

Two Avro Shackleton aircraft at RAF Scampton in 1953. The plane at the top of the picture has its radar antenna lowered into its operating position. (RI–942)

Royston Clarke's Memories

Royston Clarke remembers his days at Ludford Magna.

RAF Ludford Magna was situated at almost the highest point in the county, but despite its altitude, it was very muddy and soon earned the nickname 'Mudford Magna'.

Royston Clarke was posted there with 101 Squadron in 1943 and tells of his time there until he was shot down over Germany on his 30th mission. He now lives in retirement at Wragby, but still makes return nostalgic visits to the old airfield.

After our crew finished operational training, we were praying that we would go on to a Lancaster squadron and when it came through that we were going to Ludford Magna, we checked and found that they were flying Lancasters, because someone told us they were Stirlings, when we arrived there, the whole crew together, we saw the Lancasters and we went absolutely mad! They were only just coming in then, in June 1943, when Ludford Magna opened, we arrived there towards the end of the month.

When we walked across the airfield, there was no transport, all of the crews walked across, we thought it was a joke, we honestly thought that this is not an operational airfield, there were workmen everywhere, there were Nissen huts going up. We just couldn't believe it was a squadron. And then they told us where the headquarters were, and that wasn't completely built. We didn't like it at all. To tell the truth, I thought about going back home but after getting to know Ludford Magna it was a marvellous place, ground crews and air crews just put up with it, pulled and worked together 'For King and Country'.

We thought 'It will be OK.' It was such thick mud, when we went home, we put sacking round our shoes to keep them clean, it was awful, but it turned out a nice place in the end.

After we were there a while, they showed us around the squadron. They weren't doing Ops at that particular time, the aircraft and crews were flying in, and I could just not believe how organised it was. It was just like a town. We had our own hospital, butchers, bakery, cinema, all being completed – every single thing we wanted, we didn't have to go out, everything was at Ludford Magna. But the only thing which shook us up was when the CO gave us a lecture. "Now I want to tell you, you are going to be aircrew here, this is going to be a good squadron." We said "Oh yes, we know that Sir." He continued "I want you to know that a Lancaster costs £40,000. Never lose one. And to replace an engine, if you get shot up, that's £2,500." Then he told us how much each part cost. He said a Bren Gun cost £25.

We could defend Ludford Magna from the enemy. We had searchlights, anti-aircraft guns, Bren Guns, all the crews trained to use them, in case we were attacked, because at that particular time, we weren't doing very good in the war. We were the only country that was taking the war to the enemy. We did circuits and bumps, we lost a few crews on that, but the biggest shock of all was when I started out on my first raid; it was Peenemünde, the V-1 rocket site, I should have been nervous but I wasn't. It was the talk about "don't lose a Lancaster, they cost £40,000" that helped. From then on, after a couple or three raids, they got all the aircrews in and said what we want to tell you is from now on you are a special secret squadron, there are no photographs to be taken, of any aircraft, when the new ones came in; they had different aerials to what the planes normally had, the loop aerial and the trailing aerial, but these had got other aerials under-

Royston Clarke's favourite aircraft, a Lancaster bomber.

neath and being a radio operator, I asked what they were for and was told that they couldn't tell us that.

Then the CO told us it was to be a special squadron and there would be an extra member of the crew, who would be German-speaking and give the wrong information to the Germans and also jam their radio so that they couldn't plot us. We thought that was a good thing but we didn't really know what was going to happen. The Germans could see through that later on and we had to do every single raid with each of our special bombers dispersed throughout the bomber stream at intervals giving this false information and we were protecting the bomber stream.

And if you are a special squadron, you know you were going to get shot up, anything special during the war was not good. Once, when coming back from Munchen Gladbach, we were attacked over base and crashed on the runway.

Ludford Magna was so special, there were 2,500 personnel, 250 were aircrew and every night when we went on Ops, the WAAFs used to pack up 250 sandwich packs for us on our raid.

We had what they called FIDO (Fog Investigation Dispersal Organisation), It was a good thing for us on foggy nights, but sometimes we had the wrong kind of fog at Ludford; FIDO wasn't a failure, but the fog at Ludford was more often than not low cloud and FIDO was designed for ground fog. Whenever we had fog at Ludford, we were usually diverted to Lindholm, Scampton or Waddington. It wasn't a success in the wrong fog, but with ground fog, it was good.

Our planes were equipped with what was called ABC, which was officially known as Airborne Cigar, technical radio equipment for receiving and transmitting German signals and then jam them with noise from a microphone mounted in one of our aircraft's engines.

There were no photographs or stories allowed of these planes because of their special equipment. The public or the rest of the country, didn't know how important 101 Squadron was. We did a raid on Mont Cenis tunnel, in the Alps, between Italy and France, and I have never read anything about it. I was on the raid, the Germans were coming through

the tunnel, and we bombed both ends. It was a moonlit night and we never even saw a night fighter. All our crews got back safely.

On my 30th raid, we were the first aircraft up and we booked our meal, and paid for it, ready for our return but we never got it, or the money back. We were picked up by a RADAR boat and our port engine was shot away. We could have turned back, but we carried on with three engines and we were only at 15,000 feet when we got over Berlin, the other planes were at 21,000 feet and being late, we were picked up by the master searchlights in no time at all.

We were 'shot to hell'. The pilot was killed, and we had no second pilot. I could fly the plane and took it over, the navigator was still alive. We planned coming straight back, at 4,000 feet below their RADAR and crash land it at Skegness or Mablethorpe, on the beach. I had flown the plane before, but never landed it so I planned to throttle back and crash land it with the undercarriage up.

But as we got out of Berlin, another plane came in and attacked us and I swerved the Lancaster and the whole plane blew up. Half of the crew were killed but a couple of us got out. I was lucky and tried to get out of the country by hiding under a troop train on the outskirts of Berlin. There was loads and loads of steam and with my flying clothing, I was quite warm, but the train went on and on and it soon became

Royston Clarke in his RAF days.

very cold. So I got out and climbed into a truck and it took me miles out of Berlin almost to the border.

I stole a bike but went round a roundabout the wrong way and got caught by this man. I told him I was a French worker. He was a Frenchman, working for the Germans, and I got caught. Then I went to Frankfurt and on to Poland. A couple of us escaped from a forced march and got back to our troops as they crossed the Rhine. On the way, we saw this German, who we had mistaken for one of our lads. I had a knife and I didn't know whether to cut his throat or not, but I couldn't do it so I kicked his backside as hard as I could and then took him prisoner until our troops came by. They treated us like kings and we arrived back home in time for Victory Day.

In Memoriam

Oh! I have slipped the surly bonds of Earth
And danced the skies on laughter-silvered wings;
Sunward I've climbed and joined the tumbling mirth of sun-split clouds…
Put out my hand, and touched the face of God.

Pilot Officer John Gillespie Magee
412 Squadron, Royal Canadian Air Force.

John Magee was a 19-year-old American, who was serving with 412 Squadron, at RAF Digby, when he was killed flying a Spitfire on 11 December 1941. He was buried in the village burial ground at Scopwick.

His poem, High Flight, is a fitting tribute to all airmen who have lost their lives in the service of their country and this section of *Big Skies Over Lincolnshire* is also intended as a memorial to them. It shows just a few of the many memorials around the county and these can be found not just at airfield sites but also in many towns and villages.

'Went the day well?
We died and never knew.
But well or ill, for freedom.
we died for you.'
Anon.

The propeller memorial at Bardney.

Bardney

The memorial to 9 Squadron, which was stationed at RAF Bardney, takes the form of a three-bladed propeller and spinner mounted on a brick base. Set into the base is a stone from Norway recalling the role of the Norwegian resistance in the squadron's attack on the German battleship, Tirpitz and bears the inscription 'Scorpion Käfjord'.

Originally dedicated in October, 1982, the memorial was moved a short distance to its present site in 1992.

The inscription on the memorial reads:

IX Squadron RAF
In memory of all ranks killed or missing
1939-1945
The Squadron flew from Honington, Suffolk
1939-1942, Waddington 1942-1943
& from Bardney, 1943-1945

Cherry Willingham's village sign.

Cherry Willingham

The name sign on the village green at Cherry Willingham incorporates a picture of an Avro Lancaster flying over the Church of St Peter and St Paul, in the village. This reflects the village's links with nearby RAF Fiskerton.

Skellingthorpe

Skellingthorpe's carved wooden village sign shows scenes from the village with an Avro Lancaster flying over. Near to the sign is a brick built memorial with flower beds. The bricks are in the colours and design of the RAF roundel. It is dedicated to Nos 50 and 61 Squadrons, who served at RAF Skellingthorpe, the site of the airfield now being part of the Birchwood Estate, at Lincoln.

The carved sign at Skellingthorpe.

Upton and Kexby

Behind the panelling of a wall, in the old village hall which served the villages of Upton and Kexby, a painting was discovered on the original walls of the building.

This depicted an aircraft flying over a typical Lincolnshire countryside scene which was no doubt intended to represent nearby RAF Sturgate, which opened as a No1 Group airfield in March 1944. It was used for training purposes, but received operational squadrons, No 50 and 61, which later moved to Waddington.

Sturgate was one of four Lincolnshire airfields to be installed with FIDO, the fog dispersal equipment. After the war, the airfield was used by the United States Air Force until 1964.

When the village hall was demolished, to make way for a new building, the wall and painting was removed and installed in the Battle of Britain Memorial Flight visitor centre, at RAF Coningsby.

Visitors to Upton and Kexby look at the painting before its removal to RAF Coningsby.

East Kirby

One of many memorials at the Lincolnshire Airfield Heritage Centre, on the former East Kirkby airfield, used by the RAF in the war and afterwards by the USAF, is a stone, situated on the site of the former guardroom.

At the top of the stone is a Lancaster bomber in plan and the inscription reads:

> *In memory of*
> *those who gave*
> *their lives with*
> *57 and 630*
> *Squadrons*
> *1939-1945*

East Kirkby's memorials at the entrance to the heritage centre.

Surrounding the memorial is a low metal fence with a Lancaster featured on the front and the squadron numbers on the sides.

Two additional plaques bear an inscription and the poem 'Old Airfield', written by a member of 630 Squadron.

The heritage centre, opened by brothers Harold and Fred Panton, in memory of Bomber Command and also their brother Christopher, who lost his life while flying with 433 Squadron, also contains a pair of stained glass windows.

These show various aspects of 617 The Dam Busters Squadron.

One panel shows Wing Cmdr Guy Gibson, Barnes Wallis, Lincoln Cathedral and the breached German Dams. The other panel depicts aircraft flown by 617 Squadron; the Avro Lancaster, de Havilland Mosquito, English Electric Canberra, Avro Vulcan and Panavia Tornado. The window commemorates the fiftieth anniversary of the squadron.

The memorial panels at East Kirkby.

Faldingworth

In All Saint's Church, at Faldingworth, there is a memorial plaque, dedicated on April 29, 1995, to the members of the Polish Air Force who served at RAF Faldingworth from 1944 to 1947.

In the spring of 1940, RAF Faldingworth was officially Toft Grange, a decoy site where half-a-dozen wooden Whitley bombers were placed as a decoy to fool the enemy into thinking that the RAF was stronger than it was.

In February 1944, 300 Squadron arrived at Faldingworth to train Polish crews, who not only learned to fly Lancasters but meanwhile, flew in their Wellington bombers on minelaying operations.

The plaque dedicated to Polish airmen is carried into Faldingworth church, accompanied by squadron standards.

The squadron's first mission with Lancasters was an attack on marshalling yards at Rouen, before the Normandy landings.

300 Squadron was disbanded in October 1946 and replaced by a second Polish squadron, 305, but it too was disbanded the following year.

The plaque depicts the Polish Air Force ensign and carries the inscription:

Polskie Sily Powietrzne

In remembrance of the many men and women of the Polish Air Force who served at Faldingworth aerodrome from 1944 to 1947

Their sacrifice and endeavour in the cause of freedom forms a bond between our two countries that will always be recalled with honour and with pride

Polska – Wielka Brytania Za Nasza I Wasza Wolnosc

Laughterton

The memorial on the village green at Laughterton is not to a squadron, but to the crew members of two aircraft which crashed near to the village.

It takes the form of a single propeller blade and reduction gear mounted on a stone cairn and there are two plaques. One bears the inscription:

In memory of F/O G C Brown RCAF, Sgt J. Corless RAF Crew of Lancaster LM292 from 103 Squadron RAF Elsham Wold killed in action near Fenton 8 August 1944
On sun tipped wing they loved to fly
Into the wide unmeasured sky.

The other reads:-

In memory of F/O F S Bradbury RAF (VR), F/O G.W. Rankin RAF (VR), F/O W.R. Clayton RAF (VR), Sgt W.H. Miller RAF (VR), Sgt J.A. Micallef RAF (VR), Crew of Short Stirling EH940 based at RAF Winthorpe, killed in action at Kettlethorpe 21 June 1944

A memorial to the crews of two aircraft which crashed near to Laughterton.

Metheringham

Located on the old airfield at Metheringam Heath is a memorial to the airmen and airwomen who served with 106 Squadron from 1939 to 1945. It takes the form of a brick 'fireplace' with memorial stones inset, in front of which are circles of coloured stone chippings in the form of an RAF roundel. The stone in the middle of the memorial is from the original memorial at Metheringham and carries the dates 1917-1919 and 1938-1946 with the motto 'Pro Libertate' (For Freedom).

Around the dedication are the names of the four bases where the squadron served, Metheringham, Finningley, Syerston and Coningsby. The memorial was dedicated on 8 July 1992.

Another plaque reads:

Dedicated to the
Airmen and Airwomen
of the
British Isles and
Dominions
Europe and America
who served on and
with
106 Squadron
in World War Two
1939-1945.

995 gave their lives
Lest We Forget

106 Squadron memorial at Metheringham.

Scampton

In the churchyard of St John the Baptist's Church, at Scampton village, is a Commonwealth War Graves Commission Cross of Sacrifice, and a sizeable number of headstones, in neat rows, marking the graves of airmen from nearby RAF Scampton, who lost their lives in World War II.

There are also headstones on the graves of German airmen whose plane crashed nearby. One stone carries two names. The extra name is that of an 'unauthorised crew-member' who had flown on the plane.

Cross of Sacrifice at Scampton.

Neat rows of memorial stones at Scampton church.

Birchwood

A memorial stone dedicated to numbers 50 and 61 Squadrons is located adjacent to the Birchwood Community and Leisure Centre, on Birchwood Estate, Lincoln, the site of the former RAF Skellingthorpe.

The polished stone obelisk carries plan views of an Avro Manchester, Avro Lincoln and a Handley-Page Hampden.

On the front, beneath the badges of the two squadrons are the inscriptions:

*To the memory of the
air crews and ground staff
who gave their lives
whilst serving with
No 50 Squadron and No 61 Squadron
5 Group Bomber Command
the Royal Air Force
2nd World War, 1939-1945*

*To live in the hearts
of those we love
is not to die*

Marshal of the Royal Air Force, Sir Michael Beetham lays a wreath of poppies on the memorial at Birchwood on 3 July 1989, at the unveiling and dedication ceremony.

Waddington

A reunion beneath the clock, in the village of Waddington, for former members of 463 Squadron and 467 Squadron. The clock, together with a plaque on a low sloping brick wall, was dedicated on 10 May 1987, and is in memory of those who died serving with 5 Group, Bomber Command.

The village sign depicts many aspects of life in Waddington and includes a Maurice Farman Shorthorn biplane, Avro Lancaster, a Royal Flying Corps cap badge, RAF Waddington station badge, the clock and plaque and an Avro Vulcan flying over the village.

Waddington's village sign with its reminders of the nearby RAF station.

The 1995 reunion beneath the clock at Waddington.

Woodhall Spa

One of the largest memorials in the county, to the Royal Air Force, comes in the form of a huge stone representation of one of the breached dams. On the spillways of the 'dam' is the Roll of Honour carrying the names of those who lost their lives.

Nearby is a stone which has been removed from RAF Scampton, where it stood over the grave of 'Nigger', Wing Commander Guy Gibson's dog, which was the mascot of 617 Squadron. It died when hit by a car and buried at midnight during the raid on the dams.

The memorial is to 617 Squadron, The Dam Busters and carries the squadron badge and the inscription:

They died for your freedom
his memorial commemorates the sacrifice of
204 aircrew of 617 'Dam Buster' Squadron RAF
in the Second World War 1939-1945
Erected by their comrades and dedicated on 17th May, 1987

617 Squadron memorial at Woodhall Spa.

The memorial to Guy Gibson's dog.

Hemswell Cliff

At the former RAF Hemswell base, now Hemswell Cliff trading estate, there is a memorial to all who served at RAF Hemswell from 1936 to 1967 and takes the form of a large stone plinth surmounted by an eagle. At the dedication ceremony, the City of Lincoln Lancaster, from the Battle of Britain Memorial Flight flew over the memorial.

The Lancaster bomber flies over RAF Hemswell's memorial.

Fiskerton

A rough-hewn stone memorial to members of 49 Squadron and 576 Squadron was placed on the former Fiskerton Airfield and a tree planted on 21 May 1995. The inscription reads:

This stone and tree are
sited on the airfield
in memory of those
who served here during
World War II

It also bears a plan view of an Avro Lancaster.

The dedication service at Fiskerton in 1995.

Wickenby

At the entrance to Wickenby airfield, now used for private flying, is a memorial stone with the badges of 12 and 626 Squadrons. It carries a representation of Icarus falling on one of its faces and the inscription:

Royal Air Force Wickenby
No 1 Group Bomber Command
1943-1945
In memory of the one thousand and eighty men
of 12 & 626 Squadrons
who gave their lives on operations
from this airfield
in the offensive against Germany
and the
liberation of occupied Europe

Per Ardua Ad Astra

The Lancaster from the Battle of Britain Memorial Flight flies over the Wickenby memorial.

Cleethorpes

On the seafront at Cleethorpes is a memorial to the aircrews who flew from the former RAF North Coates (the local spelling is Cotes, but the RAF always put an 'a' in the word).

Coastal Command and Fleet Air Arm Squadrons used North Coates, as did Royal Canadian Air Force

Squadrons. Two famous names from the world of entertainment served at the base, singer Edmund Hockeridge and comedian/singer Max Bygraves. After World War II, North Coates was used for a time as the home of the first helicopter-borne air-sea rescue unit and also as a base for Bloodhound missiles.

RAF North Coates memorial on the promenade at Cleethorpes. (Picture by Nora Cooke)

Revd Victor Cooper's Memories

Sgt Victor Cooper, in his RAF uniform, in 1942.

The Revd Victor Cooper served with the Royal Air Force during World War II and was stationed at RAF Scampton for a short time before being shot down and taken prisoner in 1942, spending the remainder of the war 'a guest of the Third Reich', as he puts it. Now retired and living in Totnes, Devon, with his wife, Joy, he is Honorary Chaplain to the Aircrew Association.

In the summer of 1941, I finished my flying training at the Operational Training Unit (OTU) at RAF Cottesmore and was posted to No 83 Squadron, at RAF Scampton.

This was to be seen as a good posting because Scampton was only three or four miles from the city of Lincoln. Some bomber stations were miles from anywhere and offered very limited access to any off-duty diversions, such as cinemas and dance-halls, but Lincoln offered a great deal.

Places like the Saracen's Head pub (now long-since gone) were popular drinking places and there was a good number of them. There were several cinemas, clubs and societies, large stores, tea shops, a super 'Boots' and a good selection of churches, including a memorial church to Thomas Cooper, the chartist, author and Christian preacher. Thomas is on my family tree about the time of my great-great-grandparents, or a generation earlier. I had not known about this church until it was mentioned to me by a policeman giving me instructions on how to find an address.

Lincoln was a very busy place and its citizens were certainly giving their all to the war effort – all foundries and workshops were going full bore. It is a very fine city and has a fascinating history going back to the Roman times and including such worthies as St Hugh, with his swan and Cardinal Wolsey.

It has the Brayford, Steep Hill and the Usher Gallery, where, in 1947, in the grounds, surrounded by hosts of golden daffodils, my proposal of marriage was accepted by the girl who has now been my wife for fifty-plus years.

One of the memories that I shall always have from the days when I was flying and I am sure that this goes for hundreds of old airmen, is the sight of Lincoln Cathedral from the air. If you did a nice big circuit from Scampton, going out over the village, your down-wind leg brought you right over the city and pilots who flew the Hampden could slide back their cockpit hood and there on your left was this truly magnificent edifice.

As one stands by Lincoln Cathedral today, and look up at its great towers reaching up into the sky, one can only wonder at the vision of those men, who, centuries ago, conceived the idea of building an edifice on this awesome scale to the Glory of God. And as one goes around inside, wherever the eye falls, one is reminded that only the finest in materials and craftsmanship was good enough.

The cathedral was a material expression of men's faith: faith that God reigns as king in his universe and that all human life, all human endeavour and experience are to be seen against the abiding and unchanging truth.

As you flew over the cathedral, going out on 'Ops' you felt reassured that it was there; that it was part of England, it was good and right and no matter what happened to you, it would go on. For many, the sight of Lincoln Cathedral's three towers in the fading daylight was virtually their last and loveliest sight of England.

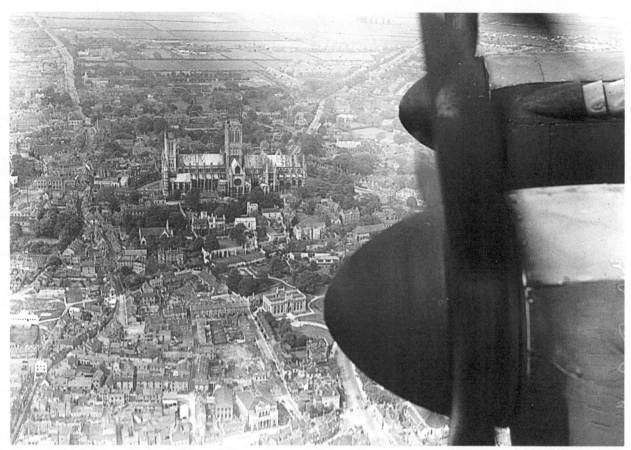

Lincoln Cathedral, the last sight of England for many airmen.

The Cathedral was part of our heritage – it belonged to us, to all of us – to the airmen flying over it and to the citizens of Lincoln down below hurrying home and putting up their blackouts.

And the inheritance was not just the stones, the stained glass and the carved oak, it was the faith which these embodied. The faith which made us all one, even with the men who built it.

Lincoln has much to be proud of and much to hand on to its citizens of the future.

Revd Victor Cooper, left, Honorary Chaplain to the Aircrew Association, at the dedication of 106 Squadron Memorial at the former RAF Metheringham, in 1992.

Orders

How to order photographs from *Big Skies Over Lincolnshire.*

Photographs in *Big Skies Over Lincolnshire* which carry a reference number can be ordered from the Photo Sales Department at the *Echo*.

Please quote the number at the end of the caption, plus the first line of the caption and page number.

Prices (including 17.5% VAT) are:

7" x 5" (18 x 12.5 cms) approx............£3.50 – Postage...75p

10" x 8" (25 x 18 cms) approx ....£5.50 – Postage...75p

16" x 12" (40.6 x 30.5 cms) approx ......£7.99 – Postage...£1.65p

No responsibility will be accepted for damage to prints sent through the post.
Cheques should be made payable to the Lincolnshire Publishing Company.

World copyright of all *Echo* photographs shall belong to the *Lincolnshire Echo.*

Photo Sales Department
Lincolnshire Echo Group Newspapers
Brayford Wharf East
Lincoln, LN5 7AT
Tel: (01522) 804342

ND - #0229 - 270225 - C0 - 297/210/9 - PB - 9781780913469 - Gloss Lamination